Fenway!

Fenway!
The Ultimate Fan's Guide

2010 Edition

Tim Shea

TBMC Press

To contact the publisher, email fenwayguide@yahoo.com.

RETAILERS AND WHOLESALERS: Bulk discounts are available. Contact
fenwayguide@yahoo.com

The text is set in Franklin Gothic Medium, Arial, and Arno Pro.

Front cover photo by Aidan C. Siegel. Used by permission of a Creative
Commons Attribution 3.0 ShareAlike License.

This book is not endorsed by the Boston Red Sox or Fenway Park.

Published by TBMC Press.

Printed in the United States of America
First printing, March 2010

ISBN 13: 978-1-438-29931-0
ISBN 10: 1-438-29931-1

10 9 8 7 6 5 4 3 2 1

For more information or to contact the author,
visit this book's blog at fenwayfanguide.com.

Contents

Introduction

Be they friend or foe of The Nation, any fan who experiences a Sox game at Fenway immediately knows they are enjoying the greatest park ever to grace the baseball landscape. The wonderfully inexplicable outfield dimensions, the fabled Green Monster, and the positively palpable scent of history tells the visitor that this certainly is the most glorious baseball home ever built, enlarged, renovated, and reinvigorated.

Opened in 1912, Fenway has been a second home to New England baseball fans for almost a century. In the late 1990s, the caretaker owners devised a plan to build a new $665 million "Fenway Park" adjacent to the real Fenway. They said renovation would be too costly and impractical, and they wanted to improve the ballgame experience for all fans by giving them access to better amenities and more comfortable seats.

Thankfully, the ownership group that purchased the team and Fenway Park for $700 million in December 2001 had the foresight and decency to discard any notions of building a new Fenway Park.

Incrementally over the past nine years the new owners, guided by the architectural wizardry of the team's former Vice President of Planning and Development Janet Marie Smith, have done a superb job renovating and enhancing the fan experience through a variety of improvements. The famous Green Monster seats and Right Field Roof Deck Restaurant are two of the most dramatic additions, but there have been countless other subtle and creative changes, including greatly improving the variety and quality of food available, and clearing out storage areas to increase the public areas away from the seating.

In July 2005 the Red Sox applied to the National Park Service to have Fenway placed on the National Register of Historic Places. The process for being added to the register can take several years.

A great benefit to the team of having Fenway Park placed on the National Register of Historic Places would be the accompanying rehabilitation tax credits from the federal government. The team is in the midst of a 10-year, $200 million renovation of the park, and if the tax credits are realized it could save the team tens of millions of dollars, according to an August 2005 article in *The Boston Globe.*

Red Sox team president Larry Lucchino has said on many occasions that the ownership's mission is to improve Fenway Park while staunchly protecting its history and character.

"It's a modernization of Fenway while still being faithful to its charms and history. I think, at the end of the day, it's going to be one of our signature accomplishments that we've been able to modernize and improve Fenway and still preserve and protect the essence at Fenway. We're pretty proud of what we've done so far. We're on the right track. It's going to get bigger and better as we create more room," Lucchino said in October 2005.

"It is an honor to have the opportunity to protect and preserve Fenway Park," said John Henry, the team's principal owner, in March 2005. "We see how its history and charm attract people from all over the world, and how it helps connect generations within families."

What separates the current Red Sox owners from their predecessors is that they realize Fenway Park is both an irreplaceable treasure and the primary asset of their business. By investing $200 million into park improvements they are simultaneously increasing revenue through new seating and concessions. Consequently, the team has more money it can spend on player salaries, and if they make the right decisions on players, the team plays better, fans want to come to the games more than ever, and the team continues to sell out every game.

As the 2010 season approached, the vast majority of planned renovations to the park had been completed, prompting Smith to leave the team, as her mission at Fenway had been accomplished. The winter of 2009-2010 saw very minor upgrades to the park, with just some waterproofing and seat refurbishing of Grandstand sections that were not addressed the prior winter.

More than ever, Fenway is now a baseball paradise. It is a destination unto itself, and the fact that the home team is consistently good only adds to the enjoyment. The food and beverage options have been multiplied and enhanced to suit every taste. The improvements also extend beyond the walls of Fenway itself, as even the famous Cask'n Flagon, once mainly a spot to grab a cold one before, after, or instead of, a game, now smacks of gentility with its dining tables on a veranda that look out upon the back of the Green Monster.

While the improvements to the park over the past several years have astounded all observers, there is one ancient element that still causes fans consternation: the infamous poles. Needed to support the park's second level, which now includes the press box, luxury boxes, pavilion seating, and the tony new EMC Club, the poles at Fenway are legendary for their ability to make you move backward, forward, and sideways in your seat so you don't miss key moments of the action.

There are many different types of seats at Fenway Park: Field Box, Loge Box, Right Field Box, Grandstand, Bleachers, Green Monster seats, Right Field Roof Deck Restaurant seats, and more. However, it is only the Grandstand Seats that have poles between the fans and the action on the field. Since most of the box seats are owned by season ticket holders, the average fan most often finds himself buying Grandstand or Bleacher seats. Some of the seats that are located behind poles are marked Obstructed View; others may not be.

In addition to providing useful information about how to get the most out of your Fenway experience, this book will help you identify those seats that have a pole impeding the view of home plate or the pitcher's mound, which is where the average fan's attention is focused during the majority of a game. Some fans may be surprised to learn that only about 3 percent of all the Grandstand seats have significant pole issues. That statistic, however, is not likely to be very comforting to the fans sitting behind a pole.

Some Facts about the Poles

- ◆ There are 26 steel poles positioned between the Loge Box and Right Field Box seats (red) and Grandstand seats (blue).
- ◆ Each pole is painted green and is about 16 inches wide.
- ◆ They are evenly spaced around Fenway, from sections 1 to 33.

Another valuable feature of this guide is the last chapter "How Far from the Field are my Seats?" The section and row numbering at Fenway Park can be very confusing if you are not in the park and are merely looking at a ticket that says your seat (or the seat you are considering purchasing) is in Right Field Box 89, row GG, for example. This quick and easy-to-use chapter lets you know that your seat is in the right field corner, behind Box 86, and is 16 rows from the field. **Using this chapter, you can determine the distance from the field for every row in the main seating bowl.**

Fenway Park Renovations

The Red Sox ownership and management have done a phenomenal job renovating and improving Fenway Park since buying the team in December 2001 for $700 million. They are now in the latter stages of a 10-year renovation plan that is expected to be completed in time for the park's 100th anniversary in 2012. Some of the highlights of the renovations, which have been led by architect Janet Marie Smith, include creating multiple new eating and gathering areas for fans, building new seating areas in very creative places, and increasing the park's capacity by 10% to just fewer than 40,000.

The Red Sox have done all of this with careful regard for the park's status as a potential national landmark, and changes are made in accordance with the standards set by the National Park Service and are reviewed in advance by the Massachusetts Historic Commission, the Boston City Landmarks Commission and Boston Redevelopment Authority. The team also consults regularly with neighborhood groups and fan advocacy groups like Save Fenway Park before making changes.

Year I – 2002 Season

With only a few months between the purchase of the team in December 2001 and Opening Day in April 2002, the ownership did not have time to make any major changes to the park in the first year. One of their first moves was to begin planning for the future by hiring architect Janet Marie Smith, who had worked with Larry Lucchino in Baltimore in the early 1990s on the construction of Oriole Park at Camden Yards. The modest physical changes to the park included adding two rows of field-level seats behind first base and third base. These seats would become known as Extended Dugout Box seats.

The Yawkey Way Concourse was also created by simply placing turnstiles at Gates A and D several hours before game time. This allows fans the use of Yawkey Way during the entire length of the game, and new concession stands have been built outside the park on the street. The original intent was to give fans a place where they wouldn't feel as cramped as they might in the packed ballpark, and then in ensuing years the team proceeded to continue to alleviate congestion by opening up numerous areas that had been cramped to make them more spacious and comfortable.

Year II – 2003 Season

Perhaps the most noticeable change to the entire park in the 10-year plan was achieved early on – the creation of the Monster Seats above the left field wall. Three steep rows of barstool seats and counters were built and they quickly became the hottest off-the-field topic in baseball. There are about 275 seats plus standing room tickets for

The Monster Seats have three rows, plus a standing room area in back.

this section. While the Red Sox have done a good job keeping ticket price increases modest for most seats in the park, the face value of the wildly popular Monster Seats has increased from $50 in 2003 to $165 in 2010.

In addition, two rows of seats were built in front of the Field Box seats between the two dugouts. Known as Infield Dugout Box Seats, they have a face value of $328 each.

A huge improvement for most fans was the expansion of the concourse in the right field and bleacher areas. This helped greatly ease the congestion for fans when they leave their seats to go to the concession stands or the bathroom. It also allowed for the creation of numerous new food and beverage options, and picnic tables were installed in an open-air concession area.

Year III – 2004 Season

The second-most famous addition to the park – the Budweiser Right Field Roof Deck Restaurant – was added this season. In an area that used to be only used occasionally for the taping of a NESN pre-game show, the Red Sox built a bar and restaurant with about 60 tables shaped like home plate, with each table seating four people. The tickets to these tables are sold through an online lottery in late winter and fans must buy a table with four seats. The ticket price of $115 per seat includes a $25 food allowance. Fans who sit here can enjoy higher quality and more diverse food options than what is available elsewhere in the park, complete with wait service.

The Right Field Roof Deck also features a standing room area (special tickets required, also sold through the lottery) and a covered bar. The bar is 60 feet, 6 inches long on each side, and the wood used for the bar's counter was taken from the bowling lanes that used to exist under Fenway Park. The deck is also the filming location for

The Right Field Roof Deck Restaurant sits just above the retired numbers and to the right of the bleachers.

NESN's speed-dating show, *Sox Appeal*.

Other improvements for the 2004 season included: widening the concourse and entrance at Gate E, which is located just to the left of the Green Monster and across the street from the Cask'n Flagon; adding new signage in the seating areas to make it easier to find your seats; and erecting a Ted Williams statue outside Gate B on Van Ness Street.

Year IV – 2005 Season

On March 23, 2005, while still basking in the Red Sox first World Series championship in 86 years, the team's ownership announced its intention to remain in Fenway Park for at least a generation to come. Up to this point the Red Sox had been making improvements to the park while simultaneously conducting a study of the feasibility of making a long-term commitment to playing baseball in Fenway Park.

The off-season improvements this year were not as noticeable as the past couple of years, but they did include a major overhaul of the Red Sox's clubhouse, plus the construction of a new batting tunnel under the first base dugout and a new weight room. The concourse behind the first base grandstands was expanded to make room for more concessions and places for fans to mill around, and a restaurant/club named Game On! was opened at the corner of Brookline Avenue and Lansdowne Street.

Year V – 2006 Season

Team president and CEO Larry Lucchino calls the improvements for the 2006 season "the largest renovation in the history of Fenway Park."

The changes included removing the soundproof glass from what used to be called the .406 Club behind home plate and splitting that seating area into two sections, a lower section called the EMC Club and an upper section called the Home Plate Pavilion Club. The glass barrier between the fans and the rest of the park had long been criticized for distancing the fans in that area from the game.

The Home Plate Pavilion Club connects on the same level with the State Street Pavilion Club areas, which extend out down the first and third base lines. The area of the State Street Pavilion Club was formerly known as the Infield Roof Boxes.

The visual effect of these changes to the second level was that they began to improve the look of a rather haphazard and inconsistently designed group of connected seating areas, changing the second level into something more elegant and symmetrical. The improvements to the second level would continue for the next few years, with the construction of the Left Field Pavilion Reserved seats in 2008 and the replacement of the Right Field Roof seats in 2009.

In the biggest capacity jump in decades, the Red Sox built 1,500 new seats (1,000 behind home plate) to bring the park's capacity to 38,805, including standing room. In addition, a new sound system was installed in the park. Unfortunately, the team often uses the system to play loud rock music between innings, a feature many fans find unnecessary and intrusive.

Year VI – 2007 Season

After a major renovation to the park's second level in 2006, the renovations for 2007 were relatively modest and scattered throughout the ballpark.

The most noticeable change was the expansion of the concession area and the creation of a standing room area behind the grandstand sections down the left field line. To accomplish this, the team took down a wall that was behind the grandstand sections and opened up several thousand square feet of space for concessions and a standing room area to watch the game. For this to happen, it was necessary to move NESN's offices from Fenway Park to Watertown, a suburb of Boston.

A new batting cage for the visiting team was built under the third base seating areas. This was important because the old batting cage was under the centerfield bleachers, and with that space becoming available, the team would start construction on the Bleacher Bar, which would open in May 2008.

Other changes included the renovation of 26 luxury suites, and building code improvements such as the installation of sprinklers throughout the park and new power lines.

Year VII – 2008 Season

The main improvement for 2008 was the construction of the Left Field Pavilion Reserved section, also known as the Coca-Cola Corner. This area of 412 seats has about 10 rows and basically extends the State Street Pavilion on the second level from third base all the way out to the Green Monster. In addition to the new seats, an area with picnic tables and more concessions was built behind the seats.

The seats in this area are topped with a 42-foot-long and 12-foot-high lighted, scrolling Coca-Cola logo sign. The installation of this sign coincided with the removal of the three 25-foot high Coca-Cola bottles that had been affixed to the light tower above the Green Monster from 1997 to 2007. These bottles were actually created for the 1996 Olympics in Atlanta.

All 6,500 seats in the bleachers were also removed and the concrete below the seats was waterproofed. New seats were installed and the old seats were then sold for $495 a pair to season ticket holders and $550 a pair to the general public.

The much-anticipated Bleacher Bar opened under the centerfield bleachers on May 16, 2008 with Larry Lucchino pouring the ceremonial first beer. The bar and restaurant is open year-round and features a view onto the field through the garage door in center field, which is about 14 feet wide and 10 feet high. This unique space lets fans eat and drink while enjoying a view of the park anytime during the year, even during ball games. During games (and when it is cold), a window with one-way glass is lowered over the opening so the bar does not become a distraction to the players. The menu consists mainly of sandwiches, and the Bleacher Bar is run by the Lyons Group, a restaurateur that operates many of the restaurants and nightclubs around Fenway.

Year VIII – 2009 Season

The 383 Right Field Roof Box seats were removed and replaced with 560 new seats to make the seating down the right field line look similar to the seats in the Left Field Pavilion Reserved section, which opened in 2008. In order to do this, the bleachers in Conigliaro's Corner were removed after two years of use. In addition, 28 seats were added to the Budweiser Right Field Roof Deck restaurant. The new seating, as well as improvements to the concession and standing room areas in right field, completes the work done on the park's second level.

In the main level, the waterproofing of the concrete seating bowl began with the removal of all seats in between the dugouts. Seats in Grandstand sections 14 through 28 and the Loge Box and Field Box seats in front of those sections were all removed, and the Loge and Field Box seats were sold to fans, with new seats being installed in those sections. In keeping with the team's motto of preserving and protecting Fenway Park's tradition, the wooden grandstand seats (which date back to 1934) in sections 14 through 28 were removed, refurbished, and then put back into place. Fenway's Grandstand seats are the last remaining wooden seats in all of Major League Baseball. They were adjusted to meet the current standard width of 18 inches and are now self-rising, so you don't bang your knee on empty seats when walking down the aisle.

Year IX – 2010 Season

The renovations completed during the winter of 2008-2009 marked the end of any significant construction or new features to enhance the ballpark. The winter prior to the 2010 season saw the team continue some of the waterproofing of the concrete seating bowl and refurbishing of seats that were not addressed during the prior winter.

In addition, a significant amount of time was needed during this offseason to prepare the ballpark for the NHL's Winter Classic hockey game between the Boston Bruins and Philadelphia Flyers, which was held January 1, 2010 in an ice rink constructed on Fenway's infield.

Fenway Park is now prepared to host the Red Sox for another 30 to 40 years, which was the stated goal of the team's owners.

How to Get Tickets

Having a great time at Fenway is a very easy thing to do. Getting tickets to the game you want to see, however, can be very difficult, frustrating, or expensive. The Sox are the toughest ticket in baseball, having sold out every home game since May 15, 2003 and as of the start of the 2010 season, the team held the longest consecutive games sellout streak in baseball history at 550 games.

Numerous factors contribute to the scarcity of available tickets: the allure of Fenway Park itself; the incredible improvements made to the park in recent years; its capacity being one of the smallest in baseball; the increased fervor generated by the 2004 and 2007 World Series victories; and the high number of season ticket holders (there is currently a very long waiting list to buy season tickets). Combine all of that with the legendary zeal fans in New  England have for their favorite team and you begin to understand why it is such a hot ticket.

The price charged by the Red Sox for tickets actually varies from $12 for an Upper Bleacher seat to $328 for an Infield Dugout Box seat.

And while for a variety of reasons Red Sox tickets are among the highest average ticket prices in major league baseball, the team has taken steps in the past few years to keep the cost of most tickets down so average families will not be priced out of the experience of attending a Sox game at Fenway. More than half of all the seats in

Fenway are either Right Field Box, Infield Grandstand, Outfield Grandstand, or Bleachers. For 2010, prices for these tickets are $52, $52, $30, and $28 respectively, just a few dollars more than they were 5 years ago. In addition, the team continues to offer several hundred seats in the top rows of the bleachers for $12 each. While very hard to get, these tickets are certainly the best bargain in baseball.

The team's ticket pricing strategy over the past several years has been to continue to incrementally raise the prices of the most expensive seats (most of which are owned by season ticket holders), while freezing or very modestly increasing the prices of seats most often purchased for individual games. (Prior to the 2009 season, in recognition of the economic recession, all ticket prices were frozen for one year).

There are many different ways to obtain tickets, whether you buy them directly from the team at face value or from a reseller at a premium price. Of course, buying tickets directly from the team rather than a reseller will almost always be the least expensive and safest way to get tickets.

Buying directly from the Red Sox

On Sale Dates, Sox Pax, and Group Tickets

If you want to increase your chances of getting tickets you should start paying attention in early December when the team usually puts the first batch of tickets on sale. Over the last six years the team has put tickets for 20 to 25 individual games on sale about two weeks before Christmas, usually on the second Saturday in December. These tickets are always for games in April, May, and September, and they do not include Opening Day or any Yankee games. This was first done as a way to ensure sellouts of April weeknight games which are the hardest games for the team to sell out. Now that sellouts of every game seems likely for the foreseeable future, this December on

Typical Timeline for Red Sox Ticket Sales

Early December	Tickets for about 25 games in April, May, and September, as well as Sox Pax, go on sale at redsox.com and at the Christmas at Fenway event. Usually held second Saturday in December.
Late December to mid-January	Group tickets (most are sold to prior group ticket buyers, however, there is an on sale date in mid-January for new group buyers)
Late January	Tickets for rest of season, excluding Opening Day and all Yankee games (usually the last Saturday in January)
February or early March	Lotteries for: Opening Day All Yankee games Green Monster seats (all games) Right Field Roof Deck (all games)
Day of game or week of game	There are usually a few hundred tickets held back for walkup sales, online, or telephone – start checking with ticket office and online a few days before the game

sale date serves the purpose of staggering the on sale dates to give fans more opportunities, and giving fans a chance to buy tickets before the holidays so they can give them as gifts.

The tickets for this December on sale date are sold almost entirely through redsox.com, but you can also call 877-733-7699. For the past six years the team has been holding an event called "Christmas at Fenway" to coincide with the December ticket sale. During this event fans are allowed into Fenway Park to buy tickets and meet some Red Sox players and management. You can only attend Christmas at Fenway if you are chosen through an online lottery. As with any Red Sox on sale date, the vast majority of available tickets usually sell out in a day or less.

The Sox Pax are an excellent deal if you are able to get your hands on one. They consist of tickets to 4 games, with at least one or two being a highly sought after game such as the Yankees or Opening Day. There are up to 10 different game sets available, and the Sox Pax usually go on sale the same morning as "Christmas at Fenway." There are a limited number of Sox Pax available, so check redsox.com or call the ticket office (877-733-7699) in early December for more information.

Group ticket sales (20 or more for one game; total of 3 games allowed) are a great opportunity if you are able to buy them. They usually go on sale in late December or early January before tickets for most games are made available to the general public. Group sales are very limited, and due to high demand, the team has had a policy the past several years of selling the majority of group sales to people or organizations that have purchased group tickets in the past. However, they do set aside some group tickets for first-time buyers, but you need to call on a specific day to have a chance to purchase them. Call the ticket office (877-733-7699) in December or early January for more information.

Tickets for the remainder of the regular season—with the exception of Opening Day and all Yankee games—typically go on sale on a Saturday morning in late January or early February. About 40 to 45 games are available, including all the prime weekend and summer games. Tickets for this on sale date are sold mainly through redsox.com, but you can also call 877-733-7699. At the appointed time, legions of fans across New England punch up their Web browsers and sit in the "Virtual Waiting Room" for anywhere from 2 minutes to 20 hours. Many fans never make it to the spine-tingling moment when they actually see tickets offered to them on the Web site. By the end of the day or early the next morning, the Red Sox regular season is basically sold out, and fans who got nothing or didn't get the games they wanted have to look to other ways to obtain tickets.

Opening Day, Yankee games, Green Monster seats, and the Right Field Roof Deck Restaurant

Some tickets are so highly sought after that the team decided about five years ago to make the opportunity to purchase tickets to them available only through a lottery system. By doing this, they hope to increase the chances of average fans getting tickets to the best games and some of the best seats in the park. This includes all tickets to Opening Day, the 9 or 10 Yankee games each year, as well as Green Monster and Budweiser Right Field Roof Deck Restaurant tickets to all 81 home games. Through a series of staggered lottery drawings in February and early March, lucky fans that are chosen are given the opportunity to come back to redsox.com at a specific time and purchase tickets with a special passcode. Fans who are chosen are usually allowed to buy four tickets to one game.

Buying tickets during the season

Once the season begins in April there is an excellent chance that each home game could already be classified as a sellout. However, there are still some opportunities for buying tickets from the team if you are patient and persistent. Some levels of membership to Red Sox Nation, the official team fan club (redsoxnation.com), include tickets to a game or the opportunity to buy tickets. In 2010, three different Red Sox Nation fan memberships – ranging in price from $120 to $240 – guaranteed the buyer 2 or 4 tickets to a game (price of tickets was included in the membership cost). The tickets offered had a face value of approximately $30, so there is a significant surcharge, but the attraction is that it guarantees you tickets, often to a weekend summer game. For $299, a Red Sox Nation Monster pack membership included the guaranteed opportunity to purchase 2 Green Monster tickets to a game. You still have to pay for the Monster Seat tickets, which are $165 each. As with any Red Sox ticket buying opportunity, you are encouraged to act quickly if you are interested in obtaining tickets through a Red Sox Nation membership. Start checking the Red Sox Web site for information about memberships in November and December. Please note that the Red Sox Nation memberships that include tickets are often sold out by March of each year.

If you have the ability to be spontaneous and can decide to go a few days before or the day of a game, the Red Sox usually release a few hundred tickets a few days before or on the day of a game. The team does hold back tickets until a day or two before the game for various reasons, including meeting the potential ticket needs of VIPs, of visiting teams, and handicapped accessible seating. Often they have held back more tickets than are required to meet those needs and some of the remaining tickets are released one to three days before each game. Check redsox.com or call the ticket office (877-733-7699) regularly for availability.

There is no standard time or method by which the team releases tickets close to a game. Tickets are coded in the ticket office for Web sale, box office sale, phone sale, or day of game walkup sale. You are advised to check as many different types of sale as you can, and do so at different times of the day.

Day of Game Walkup Sales

It is a long-standing tradition that the Red Sox sell tickets on game day to individuals who walk up to the park. Here are the rules:

- Day of game tickets are only sold at the ticket window at Gate E on Lansdowne Street
- The team starts selling tickets 2 hours before game time, which is when the gates open for fans
- You are not supposed to line up for tickets until 5 hours before game time
- You cannot save a place in line for anyone
- Everyone who buys a ticket must be in line, and they must go into the game immediately after buying their ticket

On an average game day, the team will sell anywhere from 50 to 300 tickets through this method. And yes, you can get into Yankee games by waiting in line on the day of the game. The team often hands out numbered wrist bands to the fans in line several hours before putting the tickets on sale.

If you want to get a day of game ticket you should go to Gate C about 6 hours before game time and look to see if there is a line forming. If there is no line, you can come back a little later. Just because you are in line does not mean you will definitely get a ticket, so you want to be as close to the front of the line as possible.

Another great way to get tickets is to go to Gate B on Van Ness Street near the Ted Williams statue about 1 hour before game time. There you will find Red Sox employees monitoring the Scalp-Free Zone and coordinating transactions between fans who want to sell and buy extra tickets.

So, regarding getting tickets during the season, the message is: keep trying. Don't give up just because it appears the season is sold out and you think you may be stuck paying double face value (or more) for tickets from a reseller.

Season Tickets

The Red Sox have a season ticket waiting list. Fans can join the list for a fee of $50. There are currently more than 6,000 people on the waiting list and only a small number of new fans are given the opportunity to buy season tickets each year. Usually the fans that are taken off the list and given the opportunity to buy tickets are allowed to purchase partial ticket packages, such as tickets to weekend games only.

How to Contact the Team about Tickets

Online ordering: redsox.com
Ticket office at Fenway Park: 877-733-7699 (877-RED-SOX9)
Open Monday through Friday, 10 a.m. to 5 p.m.
24-Hour Telephone Order Line: 888-733-7696 (888-RED-SOX6)

If you have any questions about how to obtain tickets from the Red Sox, you can also contact them in the following ways:

Mail: Boston Red Sox
            4 Yawkey Way
            Boston, MA
            02215-3496

Phone: 617-267-9440

To order tickets to accommodate fans with disabilities, call 877-733-7699 (877-RED-SOX9).

Buying Tickets from Resellers

When fans aren't able to buy tickets from the team, or if they can't obtain the type of seats they desire, they often turn to resellers. To see many different tickets offered for sale for all the games, you can go to Ebay.com, Stubhub.com or any number of different online ticket brokers. To find ticket brokers, just go to Google or Yahoo and search for "Red Sox tickets." Look carefully at the tickets offered at different ticket broker sites. You will usually find that many of them are offering the same exact tickets. This is because in order to increase their available inventory, ticket brokers pool their ticket listings so they can be displayed on many different sites. Usually the prices are the same from site to site, but sometimes they are not.

There is no specific going rate for tickets, but in general you can obtain tickets at Ebay.com or Stubhub.com for about double the ticket's face value (often a lot more for Green Monster seats). Prices from professional ticket brokers tend to start higher than that, and of course, the better the seats and the more desirable the game, the higher the markup.

If you want to go to a Yankee game at Fenway, the cost of buying from a reseller can be shocking. No matter which type of reseller you look at, you are likely to find prices starting at three to five times the face value.

Keep in mind that the way the team is playing is often reflected in how much you will have to pay for tickets from a reseller. When the team is winning often and the team is in first place, prices will be higher.

IMPORTANT TIP: If you are in the Boston area and can be spontaneous the day of a game, you should check Stubhub.com the morning of a game and throughout the day to see if ticket prices start to go down. What will often happen is that there will be more tickets available from resellers than there are people who want to buy them (or pay the prices they are asking). Rather than get nothing, resellers often lower their asking price during the day of a game so they will not go unsold. Often, the prices a few hours before the game come down to or below face value. If you don't have internet access, you can also check prices on game days by calling Stubhub at 866-STUBHUB (866-788-2482).

Stubhub has an office where you can conveniently pick up your tickets just a 5-minute walk from Fenway Park at 665 Beacon St., Suite 200. They do not do walkup sales at the office; you must order your tickets online or over the phone before going to the office.

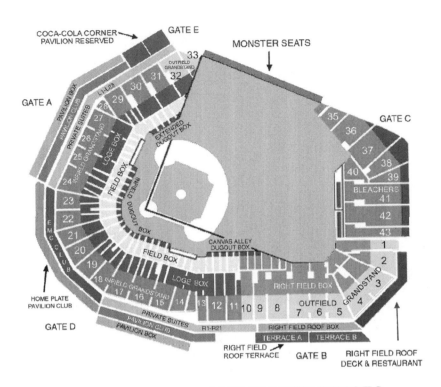

2010 SINGLE GAME TICKET PRICES

Field Box	$130
Loge Box	$95
Coca-Cola Corner	$75
Right Field Box	$52
Right Field Roof Box	$52
RF Roof Box Standing	$30
Right Field Roof Terrace	$50
RF Roof Terrace Standing	$30
Infield Grandstand	$52
Outfield Grandstand	$30
Lower Bleachers	$28
Upper Bleachers	$12
Standing Room	$20

Green Monster

Seats	$165
Standing Room	$35

Pavilion Level

EMC Club	$322
Home Plate Pavilion	$220
Pavilion Club	$170
Pavilion Box	$90
Pavilion Standing Room	$25

Right Field Roof Restaurant

1 Seat at a 4-person table	$115
Standing Room	$30

Premium On-Field Dugout Seats

Infield Dugout Box	$328
Extended Dugout Box	$274
Canvas Alley Dugout Box	$137

Types of Seating

Infield Grandstand

Face value of tickets is $52

Comprised of sections 11-31, the Infield Grandstand sections are located directly behind the Loge Box sections and they run from the middle of the right field line (Section 11) to the middle of the left field line (Section 31), forming a horseshoe around the infield.

Along with the Outfield Grandstand sections, these seats can be affected by pole obstructions. For more information on the location of the poles, see the diagrams in the second half of this book. In general, Infield Grandstand seats are the best seats the average fan can expect to be able to buy from the team. This is because the vast majority of Loge Box and Field Box seats are sold to season ticket holders. There are standing room tickets available ($20) and hundreds of fans stand behind the Infield Grandstand sections during each game. Seats in the Infield Grandstand can be affected by pole obstructions. For more information on the location of the poles, see the diagrams later in this book.

Outfield Grandstand

Face value of tickets is $30

Comprised of sections 1-10 and 32-33, the Outfield Grandstand sections are located next to the outer edges of the Infield Grandstand sections. The Outfield Grandstand sections located in right field (1-10) are some of the least sought after seats in the park due to their location and the odd way that many of the sections face center and left fields, rather than the infield. Sections 1 and 2 face the infield, but are extremely far from home plate. Sections 3 and 4 face the left field foul pole. Sections 5 though 10 are closer to home plate, but face left and center fields. If you sit in sections 5 through 10 you will spend most of the game looking to your left over the heads of hundreds of fans and it can be a pain in the neck, literally.

The sections in left field (32 and 33) are no alcohol, family sections. Seats in these two sections offer some of the best values in the park. The seats are close to the field and the Green Monster and they face the infield. Seats in the Outfield Grandstand can be affected by pole obstructions. For more information on the location of the poles, see the diagrams later in this book.

Loge Box

Face value of tickets is $95

The Loge Box sections are situated between the Grandstand and Field Box sections. They run from halfway down the right field line all the way around the infield until just before the Green Monster. Generally speaking, they offer a great view of the park.

The vast majority of these tickets are owned by season ticket holders. The Loge Box sections are in front of the poles, and only a handful of seats have any pole issues whatsoever.

One thing to keep in mind if you have the opportunity to buy Loge Box seats: the first two or three rows (AA, BB, and CC) can be affected by walkway traffic which can make it very difficult to enjoy the game. To check to see if there is a walkway near the seats you are considering buying, see the detailed Loge Box seating information beginning on page 142.

Field Box

Face value of tickets is $130

Field Box sections are located on the field from halfway down the right field line to halfway down the left field line. They are closer to the action than any other seats in the park (other than Dugout Box Seats), and they are almost all owned by season ticket holders.

Infield Dugout Box, Extended Dugout Box, and Canvas Alley Dugout Box

Face value of tickets is $328 for Infield Dugout Box, $274 for Extended Dugout Box, and $137 for Canvas Alley Dugout Box

These are all super-premium seats added in the past several years. They are directly on the field, surrounding the infield and are in front of the field box seats. In most cases there are only two rows of these seats.

Right Field Box

Face value of tickets is $52

Right Field Box sections are located in front of Grandstand sections 1 through 10. The majority of these seats are very good as they are close to the field and are reasonably priced.

Lower Bleachers

Face value of tickets is $28

The bleachers are located in center field (sections 34-40) and right field (sections 41-43). The vast majority of bleacher seats are classified as "Lower Bleachers." The bleachers have plusses and minuses. If you sit there you know you won't ever have to deal with a pole affecting your view. However, you are far from home plate and you are open to the elements, especially the sun and rain. If you get seats in Sections 40-43, you may want to get seats above the fifth row to avoid having to look through a metal screen that separates the bleachers from the bullpens. The bleachers seem to go up forever, so be assured that there is a great deal of difference in the view from bleacher row 7 vs. bleacher row 45.

Upper Bleachers

Face value of tickets is $12

The Upper Bleacher sections 36-43 are located in the last 5 to 10 rows of each of those sections, usually at least 40 rows up. The team introduced these lower-priced bleacher seats about 5 years ago as a way to offer some seats in the park at a very affordable level. The $12 price has held steady for several years. Not surprisingly, at this price and with a relatively small quantity available, they are some of the first tickets to be sold.

The Upper Bleacher seats are further from home plate than any other seats in the park, but being so high up, they often are treated to cool breezes on hot days.

Green Monster

Face value of tickets is $165

Introduced several years ago to a tremendous amount of fanfare, the Green Monster seats are some of the most expensive and highly sought after seats in the park. There are only about 275 Green Monster seats, and given the love Sox fans have for their famous green wall, it is easy to understand why they are so popular. The seats are only sold through a special preseason ticket purchasing opportunity that usually occurs in February or March. Go to redsox.com in January or February to enter a drawing to be eligible for the opportunity to purchase tickets. There are standing room tickets available for $35, and these are sold to fans selected in the same drawing.

EMC Club

Face value of tickets is $322

Opened in 2006, the EMC Club replaced the .406 Club. Unlike the .406 Club these seats directly behind home plate are open to the elements as the glass windows were removed over the winter. At $322 a ticket it is unlikely that the average fan will ever watch a game from the EMC Club unless someone gives him a ticket.

Home Plate Pavilion Club

Face value of tickets is $220

Located above the EMC Club, these exclusive seats are also sold to season ticket holders. Another new section for 2006, these seats provide a great view of the field, but the cost is prohibitive for the average fan.

State Street Pavilion Club

Face value of tickets is $170

These seats just above the first and third base lines are located in the spot where the seats used to be called infield roof box seats. Opened in 2006, they are excellent seats for viewing the game.

Pavilion Box

Face value of tickets is $90

These seats just above the first and third base lines are located above the State Street Pavilion Club seats. Opened in 2006, they are part of the revamping of the upper level that took place in the winter of 2005-2006. Standing room tickets for this section are available for $25.

Coca-Cola Corner Pavilion Reserved

Face value of tickets is $75
Construction on these seats began immediately after the Red Sox won the 2007 World Series. They extend out from the State Street Pavilion Club and Box seats on the third base line and almost reach the Green Monster. The new seats are all in Pavilion sections 16 and 18. They offer a fine view of the park, but fans sitting in them might be surprised at how high up they are, at 20 to 30 feet *higher* than fans sitting atop the Monster.

Right Field Roof Box

Face value of tickets is $52
Perched above Outfield Grandstand sections 5-9, these open-air seats offer a sparkling view of the entire park at a reasonable price. A new seating area with several hundred new seats was constructed prior to the 2009 season. Standing room tickets for this section are available for $30. This section is also located next to the Budweiser Right Field Roof Deck Restaurant, however, you cannot enter the Roof Deck Restaurant area unless you have a ticket for it.

Right Field Roof Terrace

Face value of tickets is $50
Located above the Right Field Roof Box seats, the Terrace was built prior to the start of the 2009 season. It offers a view similar to the Coca-Cola Corner seats in left field. Standing room tickets for this section are available for $30.

Budweiser Right Field Roof Deck Restaurant

Face value of tickets is $115

Constructed on the roof above Outfield Grandstand sections 1 through 4, the Right Field Roof Deck Restaurant has a full menu, but to eat at one of the home plate-shaped tables you must have tickets for them. The opportunity to buy those tickets is obtained through a drawing that is usually held in February or March. Go to redsox.com in January or February to enter the drawing. The tickets are sold by the 4-person table, so you must buy four tickets for $460. The price of each ticket also includes a $25 credit towards your food bill ($100 total credit). Standing room tickets for this area are available for $30, and these are also sold to the winners of the ticket purchasing opportunity in February or March. This is also the location where they have filmed the NESN speed-dating show *Sox Appeal*.

Getting There and Parking

Most people who don't live in Boston get to Fenway by either driving or taking the "T," which is the greater Boston subway system. The official name is the Massachusetts Bay Transportation Authority, or MBTA.

Driving to Fenway Park

Driving can be a challenge, with the heavy city traffic and the difficulty you may have finding Fenway if you aren't familiar with downtown Boston.

If you do drive, there are many different approaches, but if you are coming from the north, west, or south of the city, here are some fairly simple directions:

- ◆ Take the Mass Pike (I-90) East to Exit 18-Cambridge

- ◆ Exit at Cambridge tolls and proceeds towards Cambridge

- ◆ Turn right onto Storrow Drive East (don't go over the Charles River bridge into Cambridge)

- ◆ Continue on Storrow Drive and take the Kenmore exit

- ◆ After exiting, turn right onto Beacon Street and in a few blocks you will be in Kenmore Square. Take a left onto Brookline Avenue and when you go over the Mass Pike you will see Fenway Park and several parking lots.

If you don't mind a 15-minute walk to the park, you can keep it simple by staying on the Mass Pike and getting off at Exit 22-Prudential Center and park in the Prudential Center garage. It is a 1-mile walk from the garage to the park.

If you get lost while driving, try to find your way to Kenmore Square.

Parking

There are lots ringing the park on Brookline Avenue and Boylston Street, with the biggest lot being on Brookline Avenue next to Boston Beer Works. If you park within a 5-minute walk to the park, the fee is usually $25 to $35.

See the map on page 36 for the location of parking lots closest to Fenway Park.

Taking the T

If you take the T, you want to get to the Green Line and get off at the Kenmore stop. If you are on the D branch of the Green Line you can also get off at the Fenway stop. At either stop, it is only a few minutes walk to the park.

One common way to avoid driving all the way into Boston is to go to exit 22 on I-95/128 and park at the Riverside MBTA Station. From the north or south you can simply get off at that exit. From the west you can take the Mass Pike to the I-95/128 exit 14, then go south on I-95/128 for 1 mile until you get to exit 22.

There is a 925-space parking lot at the Riverside Station. The fee to park is $5.75 and the subway fare is $2 for adults and free for children 11 and under. It is a 30-minute ride on the T from the Riverside Station to the Fenway or Kenmore station. For more information visit mbta.com or call 617-222-5000.

Taking the Fenway Tour

Touring Fenway makes a great addition to your visit to the park. The tours include access to areas that the average fan would ordinarily never see, such as the press box, and areas that can usually only be seen after buying an expensive and hard to get ticket, such as the Right Field Roof Deck Restaurant. Please be aware that the areas the tours visit vary based on what is happening in the park that day.

Tours are available 7 days a week all year long. They start hourly on Monday through Saturday from 9 a.m. to 4 p.m. and from noon to 4 p.m. on Sunday. To obtain tickets, go to the Souvenir Store on Yawkey Way, which is across the street from Gate A. The cost is $12 for adults, $10 for children under 16 and $11 for senior citizens. The tours last just about 1 hour.

On game days, the last tour begins 3 hours before the scheduled start time. The last tour of the day on game days is often abbreviated, so if you are going to a 7 p.m. night game it is recommended that you don't go on the last tour.

In addition to learning about the park's history from the guides, some of the tour stops often include:

- Green Monster seats
- the press box
- the Pavilion Club
- a walk around the field on the warning track, giving you the opportunity to take pictures in front of the Green Monster
- the dugout

If you have tickets to a 7 p.m. game and you want to make a full day of your Fenway experience, here is a suggested itinerary:

♦ take the noon or 1 p.m. tour

♦ when the tour is over, go to Gate D to watch the players come in and give the kids a chance to get autographs (2 to 4 p.m.)

♦ go out for an early dinner, see pages 38-45 for restaurant listings

♦ back to the park when the gates open at 5 p.m. to watch batting practice and settle in for the game

If you have some free time before or after the tour, you should stroll over to Kenmore Square and go to the new SupahFans Streetwear store to pick up some unique and fun Red Sox and New England sports-themed apparel and souvenirs. The store is located just a few doors down from the Hotel Commonwealth. For more information, see the complete listing for SupahFans Streetwear on page 45.

To contact the Red Sox regarding tours, call 617-226-6666, or email tours@redsox.com. You may want to call ahead to make sure the tour time you have selected has not been cancelled for that day. You can also obtain tour information at redsox.com/tours.

Restaurant and Bar Locator Map

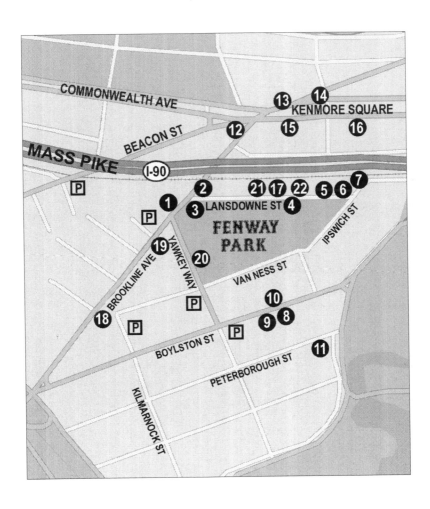

Restaurants near Fenway Park

1 Boston Beer Works

2 Cask'n Flagon

3 Game On!

4 Bleacher Bar

5 Tequila Rain

6 La Verdad Taqueria Mexicana

7 Jillian's

8 The Chicken Bone

9 Baseball Tavern

10 Jerry Remy's Sports Bar and Grill

11 Canestaro's Restaurant and Pizzeria

12 Pizzeria Uno

13 Bertucci's

14 Cornwall's Tavern

15 Eastern Standard

16 India Quality

17 The Lansdowne

Additional Bars and Nightclubs (usually not appropriate for kids)

18 Boston Billiard Club (55 pool tables), 126 Brookline Ave., 617-536-7665, bostonbilliardclub.com

19 Copperfield's, 98 Brookline Ave., 617-247-8605, copperfieldsboston.com

20 Who's On First?, 19 Yawkey Way, 617-247-3353, whosonfirstboston.com

21 House of Blues, 15 Lansdowne St., 888-693-2583, houseofblues.com/boston

22 Bill's Bar, 5 Lansdowne St., 617-421-9595, billsbar.com

P Parking Lot

Where to Eat and Drink Before and After the Game

Going to a game at Fenway can easily include a very satisfying meal just a few minutes walk to the park, thanks to a diverse array of nearby restaurants serving many different types of cuisine and fitting all budgets.

All of the restaurants listed in this section are no more than a 5-10 minute walk to Fenway. They all have menus diverse enough for kids, but the restaurants closest to Fenway (those on Lansdowne Street and Brookline Avenue) do get extremely crowded during the two hours before a game.

TIPS

♦ Visit the Web site or call the restaurant for more information

♦ If driving, try to pick a parking lot that is on the same side of the park as where you plan to eat

The restaurants in this chapter are grouped together in the following ways:

♦ Quick Bites (pages 38-39)

♦ Lansdowne Street Area (pages 39-42)

♦ Boylston Street/Peterborough Street (pages 42-44)

♦ Kenmore Square (pages 44-45)

Quick Bites
If you aren't looking for a sit-down meal with wait service, and just want to grab something inexpensive and fast, the following eateries are the places to go. All serve food that is fresh and well-prepared.

None of them are big chains, but Uburger and Boca Grande do have other locations in Boston.

Boca Grande
642 Beacon St. in Kenmore Square
617-437-9700   bocagranderestaurant.com
Burritos, quesadillas, tacos, and enchiladas—all for under $5.

Uburger
636 Beacon St. in Kenmore Square
617-536-0448   uburgerboston.com
Meat is ground on the premises and fries are hand cut with no trans fat.

La Verdad Tacqueria
1 Lansdowne St.
617-351-2580   laverdadtaqueria.com
Classic Mexican dishes with authentic ingredients. The taqueria has counter service, and next to the Taqueria is a full-service restaurant and bar with outdoor seating—see Lansdowne Street restaurant section.

Lansdowne Street Area Restaurants

Boston Beer Works
61 Brookline Ave.
617-536-BEER beerworks.net map location ➊
Just outside the park near Gate E, this lively and large restaurant and brewpub offers microbrews and a diverse menu to please any taste. If it's not too crowded (you'll often see long lines waiting to get in before a game) the variety of the food makes it a good place for kids.

Cask'n Flagon

62 Brookline Ave.

617-536-4840 casknflagon.com map location ➋

Located across the street from Fenway near Gate E, this is the oldest and most famous sports bar in the area. Serves a full menu of appetizers, sandwiches, burgers, ribs, and steaks.

Game On!

82 Lansdowne St.

617-351-7001 gameonboston.com map location ➌

This is a big-time sports bar located inside Fenway Park, just across the street from the Cask'n Flagon. You cannot enter the game through the restaurant. It features 70 high-definition TVs and its menu includes appetizers, salads, burgers, sandwiches, and brick oven pizzas.

Bleacher Bar

82A Lansdowne St.

617-267-2424 bleacherbarboston.com map location ➍

The view of Fenway Park from inside the Bleacher Bar on Lansdowne Street. The bar and restaurant is open year-round, even during games.

Located under the park's centerfield bleachers, this relatively small bar and restaurant opened in May 2008 and provides a view of the field and rest of the park through the large metal grate on the centerfield warning track. The Bleacher Bar is open year round, including during games, so fans can enjoy a nice view of Fenway any time. The location is definitely one of the main attractions, and the menu consists of American comfort foods, including corned beef, pastrami and beef brisket sandwiches, cheesy bacon fries, and warm, soft pretzels.

Tequila Rain

3 Lansdowne St.
617-437-4300 tequilarainboston.com map location ❺
Located next to La Verdad Taqueria, Tequila Rain is part of the Jillian's dining and entertainment complex. It features outdoor seating and serves Mexican and American fare including quesadillas, sandwiches, and burgers. Families should stay away from Tequila Rain at night, when it becomes a raucous bar and dance club.

La Verdad Taqueria Mexicana

1 Lansdowne St.
617-421-9595 laverdadtaqueria.com map location ❻
Authentic Mexican cuisine prepared with fresh and interesting ingredients is what you'll find here. It has interesting décor and an attractive four-sided bar. Outdoor seating is available and there is a walk-up counter next door if you are in a hurry.

Jillian's

145 Ipswich St.
617-437-0300 jilliansboston.com map location ❼
A self-proclaimed "70,000 square foot food entertainment universe," Jillian's is on the second floor of a three-story building that includes a nightclub on the first floor, Tequila Rain, and bowling on the third floor at Lucky Strike. Jillian's boasts numerous pool tables and has a

reasonably priced menu (almost everything under $10) of appetizers, sandwiches, salads, and pizzas.

The Lansdowne
9 Lansdowne St.
617-247-1222
lansdownepubboston.com
map location **17**
This new classic Irish pub occupies the space that formerly held Jake Ivory's dueling piano bar. It features a diverse menu of excellent comfort food, including a wide variety of appetizers, salads, sandwiches and burgers. It also boasts Irish favorites such as shepherd's pie, fish and chips and Guinness beef pot pie. Very good selection of tap and bottled beers. Live music many nights; shows usually don't start until 10 p.m.

Boylston Street/Peterborough Street Area

The Chicken Bone
1260 Boylston St.
877-WINGS2U thechickenbone.com map location **8**
12 varieties of wings are available in this large and fun restaurant and bar, including sticky sesame, teriyaki and thermonuclear. Expect all the classic American pub foods: burgers, ribs, subs, nachos, salads, and more. Families welcome.

The Baseball Tavern

1270 Boylston St.

617-867-8526 thebaseballtavern.com   map location **9**

A Fenway tradition, this classic Boston sports bar and restaurant has three levels, plus a roof deck that overlooks the ballpark. Serves wings, sandwiches, burgers, salads and several fish dishes.

The Baseball Tavern has been on Boylston Street for decades, although it moved one block a few years ago to make room for the construction of a condo high-rise.

Jerry Remy's Sports Bar & Grill

1265 Boylston St.

map location **10**

This new sports bar and restaurant features giant TVs, a full menu, outdoor patio seating, and the mother lode of Red Sox memorabilia. The owner is the popular TV analyst for Red Sox games on NESN.

Canestaro's Restaurant and Pizzeria

16 Peterborough St.

617-266-8997   canestaros.com   map location **11**

This charming Italian restaurant and pizzeria is tucked away in a quiet residential neighborhood a short walk from Fenway. It serves outstanding Italian food and pizza at reasonable prices and is a great spot for relaxing before or after a game.

Kenmore Square Area

Pizzeria Uno

645 Beacon St.

617-262-4911   pizzeriauno.com   map location **12**

Deep-dish Chicago style pizza, a full Italian menu, and more await at this consistently good chain restaurant.

Bertucci's

533 Commonwealth Ave.

617-236-1030   bertuccis.com   map location **13**

As their slogan says "What's Not to Love?" Very good brick oven pizza and Italian dishes.

Cornwall's Tavern

654 Commonwealth Ave.

617-262-3749   cornwalls.com   map location **14**

This friendly English pub is a neighborhood favorite, boasting a great selection of craft and imported beers, including 28 beers on tap and 80 in bottles. It is a true English pub in a city full of Irish bars. The menu includes shepherd's pie and fish and chips.

Eastern Standard

528 Commonwealth Ave.

617-532-9100   easternstandardboston.com   map location ⓯

This high-end restaurant features beautifully prepared seafood and steaks, as well as interesting appetizers such as roasted bone marrow and crispy frog's legs. Entrees are between $20 and $30. A good choice for a special date.

India Quality

484 Commonwealth Ave.

617-267-4499   map location ⓰

One diner called this restaurant a "hidden jewel in downtown Boston." It has received Zagat's Best of Boston award for Indian food and serves North Indian food with lunch meals about $8 and dinner meals from $10 to $15.

And When You are in Kenmore Square, Go To

SupahFans Streetwear

470 Commonwealth Avenue

866-SupahFans (787-2482)

For the past 5 years this popular t-shirt brand has been selling unique and creative apparel that speak to the hearts and minds of all New England sports fans through their Web site, www.SupahFans.com. Lead designer Coach Kevin and his street team started slinging SupahFan Shirts on the streets of Boston at the 2004 World Series parade and just opened their first retail store in March 2010 in Kenmore Square. Be sure to stop by their store and pick up some fun and distinctive fan wear (and more) on your next trip to Fenway. It is located just a few doors down from the Hotel Commonwealth and India Quality, in between Petit Robert Bistro (an excellent French restaurant) and Sugar Daddy's Smoke Shop.

Eating and Drinking in the Park

While the physical improvements and new seats in the park have garnered the most attention in recent years, the improvements to the quality and variety of food and beverages have probably had a greater impact on the average fan's experience. If you were sitting in Section 32, row 10 in 2000, and you sit there in 2010, your experience of watching the game has not changed much at all. However, your access to high quality food, beverages, and more comfortable areas to consume them has improved immeasurably.

It was less than 10 years ago when the fare inside Fenway was generally limited to hot dogs, sausage, french fries, and pretzels. For beer, you usually had to choose between Bud Light and Coors Light.

Fast forward to 2010 and your choices include Philly Cheesesteaks, El Tiante Cuban sandwiches, barbecued chicken, humongous hot dogs at RemDawg's on Yawkey Way, clam chowder, and more. Sushi was offered beginning in 2007 to honor the arrival of Daisuke Matsuzaka from Japan. Beer options include Sam Adams in several areas of the park, as well as Guinness, Harp, and Smithwick's, which are available near Section 19.

Since late in the 2003 season the portion of Yawkey Way that runs from Gate A to Gate D has essentially become part of the ballpark for two hours prior to and during the entire game. The team received permission from the city of Boston to close that portion of the street off so that it can be used only by fans with tickets to the game. This means that more concessions are available to fans throughout the game, including El Tiante's and RemDawg's. It also means that fans have access to the huge souvenir store on Yawkey Way during the entire game.

The areas inside the park to buy and eat your food have also been improved dramatically. A couple of years ago the team cleared out some space in right field and behind the bleachers and created a huge open-air concourse for concessions, complete with picnic tables and TV monitors to watch the game. Similarly, the left field concession area has been expanded and includes several huge plasma TVs to watch the game while you wait for your food.

Fenway Park's concession vendor, Aramark, announced in March 2007 that oils used for cooking all fried food in the park will free of trans fats.

There are also new and improved concession areas on the Green Monster and in the Pavilion sections, but you must be ticketed for those sections to get in.

The Budweiser Right Field Roof Deck Restaurant has a full menu, but to eat at one of the home plate-shaped tables you must have tickets for them. The opportunity to buy those tickets is obtained through a lottery that is usually held in February or March. Tickets are $115 each (sold only in sets of 4, so you get your own table for $460), and the price of each ticket includes $25 towards your food bill.

What all these improvements mean is that you no longer have to dine before you come into the game if you want a variety of tasty things to eat. If you want to enjoy the park when it is not crowded and catch batting practice, the gates open 2 hours prior to the scheduled start time.

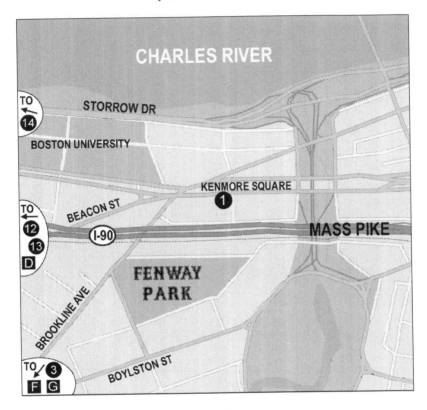

Hotels

1   Hotel Commonwealth
2   Eliot Hotel
3   Best Western Boston – The Inn at Longwood Medical
4   Hilton Boston Back Bay
5   Sheraton Boston
6   Marriott Boston Copley Place
7   Courtyard by Marriott Boston Copley Square
8   Lenox Hotel Boston
9   Colonnade Hotel
10   Westin Copley Place
11   Fairmont Copley Plaza
12   Holiday Inn Boston Brookline
13   Courtyard Boston Brookline
14   Doubletree Guest Suites Boston

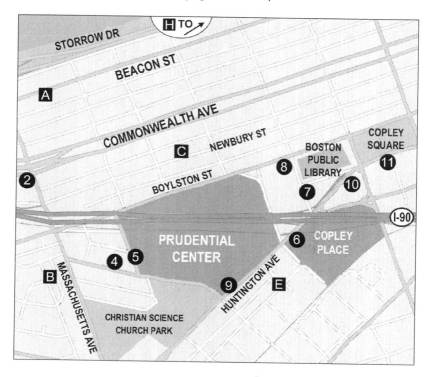

Bed and Breakfasts, Inns, and Guest Houses

- **A** 463 Beacon Guest House
- **B** Oasis Guest House
- **C** Newbury Guest House
- **D** Anthony's Town House
- **E** Copley Inn
- **F** Longwood Inn
- **G** Beechtree Inn Bed & Breakfast
- **H** The John Jeffries House

Where to Stay Overnight

Boston hotels tend to be expensive, with rooms at 3-star or better hotels often averaging $200 to $350 per night. This section will list places to stay and their key information in two ways: Hotels, beginning with those closest to Fenway Park, followed by Bed and Breakfasts, Inns, and Guest Houses.

Boston is a very popular business and tourist destination, and hotels fill up quickly. Having the Red Sox in town for a home game certainly adds to the scarcity of available rooms. You are advised to make your reservations early, as soon after you get your tickets as possible.

When considering a hotel or inn, you should check the availability and cost to park your car, and include that in your travel budget.

Keep in mind that the city of Brookline is literally just a few blocks from Fenway Park. Several of the hotels and inns listed in this section are in Brookline, as their location often makes them more convenient to Fenway than many downtown Boston hotels.

How to Save Money When you Book Your Room

Booking your room through online sites that offer you discounted rates such as Hotwire.com or Priceline.com is a great way to save a significant amount of money on your room, often up to half or more the cost of booking directly with the hotel. The reason why you can save significantly is that you must commit to purchasing a room in a hotel before you know which hotel it is. However, you are able to choose the neighborhood in Boston where you want to stay. To be closest to Fenway, choose the "Back Bay-Copley Square" neighborhood on Hotwire.com. At Priceline.com, choose "Name Your Own Price," and choose either the "Fenway Park" or "Copley Square-Theatre District" neighborhoods. At Priceline, you have to provide your credit card number and agree to pay for the room before they tell you if your offer has been accepted, so it can be a little unnerving. If you haven't used any of these sites before, you might be more comfortable with Hotwire.com.

NOTE: At both sites, be sure to choose at least a 3-star hotel or higher to help ensure you are happy with your accommodations.

Staying Outside the City of Boston

Staying in one of the Boston suburbs, such as Newton, Braintree, or Dedham has the advantage of being generally less expensive and you will usually get free parking. If you don't want to drive into the city for the game, you should talk to the hotel about the best way to get to Fenway. Some hotels will offer a shuttle to the nearest T station.

Hotels listed by proximity to Fenway Park

(Note: Two of the closest hotels to Fenway Park are the Hotel Buckminster in Kenmore Square and the Howard Johnson Fenway Park on Boylston Street. Due to the poor customer ratings these hotels received as of February 2010, they will not be listed in this section.)

Hotel Commonwealth
500 Commonwealth Ave.
617-933-5000 hotelcommonwealth.com

★★★★
Distance to Fenway: ¼ mile
Rooms: 148
Pool: no
Fitness Center: yes
Average rate: $175-$350
Map location ❶

Having just opened in 2003, this elegant hotel is the centerpiece of a revitalized Kenmore Square. The location is perfect, with many rooms looking out on the back of the Green Monster, and the park just a 5-minute walk away. The downside is that rooms can be pricey and they fill up fast for game nights.

The Eliot Hotel

370 Commonwealth Ave.
617-267-1607   eliothotel.com
This elegant hotel was voted "Best
Boutique Hotel" by Boston Magazine
in 2006, and 79 of the 95 rooms are
suites. The location is superb: less than
a 10-minute walk from Fenway and a
block from the shops on Newbury
Street. It boasts the acclaimed Clio

★ ★ ★ ★
Distance to Fenway: ½ mile
Rooms: 95, including 79 suites
Pool: no
Fitness Center: yes*
Average rate: $200-$350
Map location

Restaurant, which serves innovative Asian-influenced French cuisine, as
well as the Uni Sashimi Bar, which was named Best Sushi Bar in Boston by
Boston Magazine in 2009.

*There is no fitness center on site, but guests have access to the nearby
Boston Sports Club.

Best Western Boston – The Inn at Longwood Medical

★ ★ ★
Distance to Fenway: ¾ mile
Rooms: 155
Pool: no
Fitness Center: yes
Average rate: $160-$220
Map location

342 Longwood Ave.
617-731-4700
innatlongwood.com

Here you will find nicely appointed
rooms, a friendly staff, and reasonable
rates by Boston standards. However,
unlike most hotels in this section, the Inn
at Longwood is not within an easy walking distance of downtown Boston
attractions. However, it is an easy 10-15 minute walk to Fenway.

Hilton Boston Back Bay

40 Dalton St.
617-236-1100 hiltonfamilyboston.com

The Hilton offers what you would expect
from an upscale hotel chain: clean,
comfortable rooms, quality service, and
an indoor pool for the kids. It is a 15-
minute walk to Fenway.

★ ★ ★ ½
Distance to Fenway: 1 mile
Rooms: 385
Pool: indoor
Fitness Center: yes
Average rate: $180-$325
Map location

★ ★ ★ ★
Distance to Fenway: 1 mile
Rooms: 1216
Pool: indoor, with retractable roof
Fitness Center: yes
Average rate: $160-$325
Map location **5**

Sheraton Boston Hotel

39 Dalton St.
617-236-2000 sheraton.com/boston
The largest of the hotels in the Prudential Center/Copley Square area, this hotel features an indoor pool with a retractable roof that opens in the summer. Connected to the Prudential Center mall.

Boston Marriott Copley Place

110 Huntington Ave.
617-236-5800 bostoncopleymarriott.com

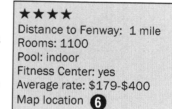

★ ★ ★ ★
Distance to Fenway: 1 mile
Rooms: 1100
Pool: indoor
Fitness Center: yes
Average rate: $179-$400
Map location **6**

Situated next to the Prudential Center, there is an enclosed walkway that gets you to all the shops in the Prudential Center mall. The rooms can be pricey, but the location, indoor pool, and Champions Sports Baron the second floor make it an attractive and comfortable place to stay.

★ ★ ★
Distance to Fenway: 1 mile
Rooms: 81
Pool: no
Fitness Center: yes
Average rate: $200 -$325
Map location **7**

Courtyard by Marriott Boston Copley Square

88 Exeter Ave.
617-437-9300 courtyardboston.com

Boston Marriott Copley Place, this boutique hotel is in a beautifully renovated building built in the late 1800s.

The Lenox Hotel Boston

710 Boylston St.
617- 536-5300 lenoxhotelboston.com

★ ★ ★ ½
Distance to Fenway: 1¼ miles
Rooms: 212
Pool: no
Fitness Center: yes
Average rate: $200-$350
Map location **8**

Located across the street from the Boston Public Library and a short walk from the Prudential Center and Copley Square, this charming hotel offers guest rooms that were beautifully renovated in 2005 and an Irish pub off the lobby.

The Colonnade Hotel

120 Huntington Ave.

617-424-7000   colonnadehotel.com

★★★★
Distance to Fenway: 1¼ miles
Rooms: 285
Pool: outdoor rooftop (summer)
Fitness Center: yes
Average rate: $150-$325
Map location **9**

This European-style hotel boasts Boston's only rooftop pool, a great spot for summer sunset cocktails with views of the city. It recently underwent a $25-million renovation that gave it a sleek and edgy look.

The Westin Copley Place

10 Huntington Ave.
617-262-9600   westin.com

★★★★
Distance to Fenway: 1¼ miles
Rooms: 803
Pool: indoor
Fitness Center: yes
Average rate: $195-$400
Map location **10**

Along with the Sheraton and the Marriott Copley, this is one of the three enormous hotels in the Copley/Prudential Center area, each with more than 800 rooms. Provides everything you would expect from an upscale hotel.

★★★★
Distance to Fenway: 1½ miles
Rooms: 383
Pool: no
Fitness Center: yes
Average rate: $195-$400
Map location **11**

The Fairmont Copley Plaza

138 St. James Ave.
617-267-5300
fairmont.com/copleyplaza

Opened in 1912 (the same year as Fenway Park) and recently renovated, this stately and luxurious hotel is one of the crown jewels of Boston. It is a great choice for couples.

Holiday Inn Brookline Boston

1200 Beacon St., Brookline
617-277-1200   holidayinn.com

Renovated in 2004, this hotel is conveniently located on Beacon Street

★★★
Distance to Fenway: 1½ miles
Rooms: 383
Pool: indoor
Fitness Center: yes
Average rate: $140-$200
Map location **12**

steps away from the St. Paul Street station of the T's Green Line. From there it is just 4 short stops to Kenmore. Reasonable rates by Boston standards — a good spot for families.

Courtyard Boston Brookline

★ ★ ★
Distance to Fenway: 1½ miles
Rooms: 193
Pool: indoor
Fitness Center: yes
Average rate: $160-$240
Map location ⓑ

40 Webster St., Brookline
617-734-1393 marriott.com

While technically located outside Boston in Brookline, this hotel near Coolidge Corner has a city feel to it. Fine restaurants and shops are just outside the door and the location near the T makes it very convenient.

Doubletree Guest Suites Boston

400 Soldiers Field Rd.
617-783-0090 doubletree.com

★ ★ ★
Distance to Fenway: 2 miles
Rooms: 305, incl. 295 suites
Pool: indoor
Fitness Center: yes
Average rate: $125-$250
Map location ⓮

Located just off eastbound exit 18 on the Mass Pike, this virtually all-suite hotel is easy to find and a 5-minute drive to Fenway on Storrow Drive.

Good spot for families, but keep in mind that it is not near a T station and not within a short walking distance of dining or shopping. The hotel runs a free shuttle to Harvard Square, Copley, and Boston Common (but not to the Fenway/Kenmore area).

Bed and Breakfasts, Inns, and Guest Houses

For those willing to depart from the predictable and usually reliable chain and large city hotels, a smaller establishment can offer a unique and memorable experience. To help ensure a pleasant stay, you are advised to do more research when booking a room at a B & B, inn, or guest house. If you reserve a room at a Marriott, for example, you can certainly make your reservation based solely on price and location: you generally know what you are going to get based on past experience at large chain hotels with good reputations. Just the opposite is true of small, family-run establishments. You should look at their Web site, read online traveler reviews at sites like tripadvisor.com, and call to speak with the owner or manager before reserving a room.

Be advised that since different travelers go into these rooms with different expectations, the opinions can vary greatly.

It is also true that Boston is one of the most historic cities in America, and many of these locations are housed in beautifully restored, century-old brownstone buildings. If you are going to Boston to bask in the history of America's greatest ballpark, why not extend that historical feel to your lodging?

Below are some common features that distinguish B&Bs, inns, and guest houses from large chain hotels. Some travelers may view some of these as positive attributes, and others just the opposite.

- there are usually only 10 to 30 rooms, so if it is a popular destination, call well in advance of your stay for reservations
- rooms at the same establishment often vary greatly in size and furnishings
- usually no pool or fitness room
- they are usually owned and run by families, and word-of-mouth advertising is very important to them, so they often do whatever they can to make you comfortable
- Guests often must share a bathroom (ask at time of booking)
- breakfast is often included (ask at time of booking)

- many require a 50% deposit or full-night's stay be paid at time of booking, and the cancellation policies are often different than traditional hotels (ask at time of booking)
- the uniqueness of a well-run and well-maintained small establishment will create many more lasting, positive memories than a typically forgettable stay at a large chain hotel.

NOTE: Most small establishments do not offer instant online reservations through their Web sites. In many cases, prospective guests need to fill out an online request form, send an email, or call the establishment. As is recommended above, you should call the inn, guest house, or B & B before making a reservation anyway. This will help you get more specific information and feel more comfortable with your choice. Another reason to call before reserving a room is that the rooms in most of these establishments are all different from one another, and photos of each room are often shown on their Web sites. By calling, you can usually select the specific room you want.

463 Beacon Guest House

463 Beacon St.
617/536-1302 463beacon.com

Distance to Fenway: ¾ mile
Rooms: 20
Average rate: $79-$149
Map location A

The self-proclaimed "Boston's Best Slept Secret" is housed in a renovated brownstone in a great location just a short walk from Kenmore Square. Web site states: "Back Bay's most inexpensive rates. Guaranteed."

Distance to Fenway: ¾ mile
Rooms: 16
Average rate: $79-$159
Map location B

Oasis Guest House

22 Edgerly Rd.
800-230-0105 or 617-267-2662
oasisgh.com

Located in a row of brownstones on a residential street, the Oasis is a short walk from Fenway Park and a multitude of shops and restaurants. Travelers give the friendly staff high marks, and guests can enjoy a cup of tea or cocktail on one of two small outdoor decks. The rooms are generally small, but very clean. Very well-liked by travelers.

Newbury Guest House
261 Newbury St.
800-437-7668 or 617-670-6000
newburyguesthouse.com

Distance to Fenway: 1 mile
Rooms: 32
Average rate: $149-$229
(breakfast included)
Map location   **C**

An historic inn housed in what used to
be three Victorian homes, the charming Newbury Guest House has a great
location and a lot of character.

Distance to Fenway: 1 mile
Rooms: 14
Average rate: $110-$150
Map location   **D**

Anthony's Town House
1085 Beacon St., Brookline
617-566-3972
anthonystownhouse.com

Housed in a beautifully restored historic brownstone on Beacon Street, the
rooms are decorated with French, Rococo, Venetian and Victorian
antiques. Travelers love the location and the wonderful attitude of the
owners. Call for information on large rooms that could accommodate a
family.

The Copley Inn
19 Garrison St.
617-236-0300   copleyinn.com

Distance to Fenway: 1 ¼ miles
Rooms: 20
Average rate: $135-$145
Map location   **E**

Housed in a brownstone on a tree-lined
street in the historic Back Bay neighborhood, this charming inn is just a
short walk from Copley Square and the T station. It offers good rates and a
great location, as well as a private bath and a kitchenette in each room. Each
room has exactly one queen bed, which makes it a good choice for couples.

Distance to Fenway: 1 ¼ miles
Rooms: 22
Average rate: $99-$129
Map location   **F**

Longwood Inn
123 Longwood Ave., Brookline
617-566-8615   longwood-inn.com

This converted Victorian mansion in a residential neighborhood just three
blocks from Boston includes rooms of varying sizes, a cozy, at-home

atmosphere, and a friendly staff. One traveler said it "felt like being away at a cottage."

The Beechtree Inn Bed and Breakfast
83 Longwood Ave., Brookline
617-277-1620 or 800-544-9660
thebeechtreeinn.com

Distance to Fenway: 1 ¼ miles
Rooms: 10
Average rate: $89-$179
Map location **G**

This quaint B &B is universally adored by travelers. The owner does an excellent job of making people feel at home and ensuring a positive stay. There are 10 distinct rooms of varying sizes and shapes, and you are able to view the exact room you will be reserving on the Web site.

Distance to Fenway: 2 miles
Rooms: 46
Average rate: $105-$175
Map location **H**

The John Jeffries House
124 David G. Mugar Way
617-367-1866 johnjeffrieshouse.com

This small hotel is further from Fenway than the other inns listed in this section, but it has many wonderful attributes: easy to find off Storrow Drive, a lot of rooms for an inn, a great location for exploring historic downtown Boston on foot, and a very charming and tasteful ambience. There are a variety of rooms and suites, so ask for specific information on your room before you book it, including the size and number of beds.

2004 Red Sox Postseason Quiz

This quiz will test your recollection of October 2004, the most memorable month in the history of the Red Sox. After completing the quiz, turn to page 66 for detailed answers.

1. Manny Ramirez held up a sign during the Red Sox World Series victory parade through Boston on October 30, 2004. What did it say?

A. I want to finish my career in Boston
B. I'm just Manny being Manny
C. Jeter is playing golf today
D. Thank you New England
E. Quo vadis, Nomar?

2. Which feeble, washed-up Yankee hurler served up a meatball to David Ortiz that he lined into the right field seats for a two-run, 1st-inning homer in Game 7 of the ALCS?

A. Tom Gordon
B. Randy Johnson
C. Mike Stanton
D. Kevin Brown
E. Mike Mussina

3. How many doubles did Trot Nixon hit in World Series Game 4?

A. 3
B. 1
C. none
D. 2
E. 4

See Answers to the Quiz on page 66

4. Which Anaheim Angels slugger gave Sox fans agita by blasting a 7th-inning grand slam into the bullpen, tying the score of ALDS Game 3 at 6-6. Ultimately, it turned out to be a blessing, as it set up Big Papi's 10th-inning heroics.

A. Tim Salmon
B. David Eckstein
C. Doug DeCinces
D. Vladimir Guerrero
E. Garret Anderson

5. Complete the call uttered by Fox-TV analyst Tim McCarver after Big Papi won Game 5 of the ALCS with an RBI single to center in the 14th inning: "He didn't do it again, did he?..."

A. ... great googly-moogly!"
B. ... he's the man of the hour with a tower of power!"
C. ... yes, he did."
D. ... never has one man done so much for so many."
E. ... give me five, I'm still alive."

6. Which Red Sox pitcher set a major league record by recording wins in the deciding games in all three postseason series in the same year?

A. Pedro Martinez
B. Curt Schilling
C. Keith Foulke
D. Derek Lowe
E. Bronson Arroyo

See Answers to the Quiz on page 66

7. Who did Keith Foulke strike out to end Game 6 of the ALCS?

A. Derek Jeter
B. Tony Clark
C. Jason Giambi
D. Alex Rodriguez
E. Jorge Posada

8. Which Red Sox player was struck in the head by a baseball thrown from the shore of the Charles River as the team floated by in Duck Boats during the World Series victory parade?

A. David Ortiz
B. Mark Bellhorn
C. Kevin Millar
D. Derek Lowe
E. Pedro Martinez

9. Game 4 of the 2004 ALCS was perhaps the most memorable game in Red Sox history. Who was the winning pitcher?

A. Keith Foulke
B. Alan Embree
C. Bronson Arroyo
D. Mike Timlin
E. Curtis Leskanic

10. Who hit a two-run homer in the 4th inning of ALDS Game 1 against Anaheim to put the Sox ahead 3-0 and send them on their way to an easy 9-3 triumph?

A. Kevin Millar
B. Manny Ramirez

See Answers to the Quiz on page 66

C. David Ortiz

D. Johnny Damon

E. Mark Bellhorn

11. Which of the following headlines did NOT appear on a New York City newspaper on October 21, 2004, the day after the Sox won the ALCS in New York?

A. What a Choke!

B. Hell Freezes Over

C. Damned Yankees

D. Yankees Stink

E. The Choke's On Us

12. How many errors did the Red Sox commit in Games 1 and 2 of the World Series combined?

A. none

B. 8

C. 4

D. 1

E. 3

13. Who hit home runs in three consecutive postseason games?

A. Manny Ramirez

B. Mark Bellhorn

C. David Ortiz

D. Jason Varitek

E. Johnny Damon

See Answers to the Quiz on page 66

14. Which overpaid Yankee superstar had only 1 hit in 17 at-bats and struck out 6 times in Games 4 through 7 of the ALCS?

A. Derek Jeter
B. Alex Rodriguez
C. Jorge Posada
D. Raul Mondesi
E. Gary Sheffield

15. Mark Bellhorn's game-winning two-run homer in the 8th inning of World Series Game 1 bounced off which fabled Fenway landmark?

A. The Green Monster
B. Dan Shaughnessy's ego
C. The Coke bottle above the Monster seats
D. Jerry Remy's mustache
E. The Pesky Pole

16. Who hit the memorable game-tying single up the middle past Mariano Rivera in the 9th inning of Game 4 of the ALCS?

A. Kevin Millar
B. David Ortiz
C. Bill Mueller
D. Dave Roberts
E. Trot Nixon

17. Which Red Sox pitcher started Game 1 of the World Series?

A. Pedro Martinez
B. Tim Wakefield
C. Curt Schilling
D. Bronson Arroyo

See Answers to the Quiz on page 66

E. Derek Lowe

18. How many saves did Keith Foulke record in the World Series?

A. 3
B. 1
C. 4
D. none
E. 2

19. Which doctor performed an experimental procedure on Curt Schilling's ankle that enabled him to pitch (and win) Game 6 of the ALCS and Game 2 of the World Series?

A. Dr. James Andrews
B. Dr. Demento
C. Dr. Arthur Pappas
D. Dr. Pepper
E. Dr. Bill Morgan

20. Edgar Renteria hit a one-hopper that was "stabbed by Foulke" and underhanded to Doug Mientkiewicz at first to end the World Series. What uniform number was Renteria wearing?

A. 4
B. 11
C. 5
D. 24
E. 3

See Answers to the Quiz on page 66

Answers to the Quiz

1. C	5. C	9. E	13. B	17. B
2. D	6. D	10. A	14. E	18. B
3. A	7. B	11. D	15. E	19. E
4. D	8. E	12. B	16. C	20. E

Detailed answers:

1) C. Jeter is playing golf today
A fan on the parade route handed the sign to Manny, and he happily displayed it throughout much of the rolling rally.

2) D. Kevin Brown
Brown was a horrible choice to start a deciding Game 7, having recently rejoined the team after breaking his hand punching a wall. But with games on 5 consecutive days, including 2 extra-inning classics, Joe Torre didn't have many options.

3) A. 3
Trot Nixon had a disappointing 2004 regular season. Hampered by injuries, he had only 149 at-bats. But the original Dirt Dog came through in the deciding game of the World Series, smacking three doubles and driving in two runs.

4) D. Vladimir Guerrero
Guerrero's dramatic 7th-inning grand slam was one of the only bright spots in the series for the prodigious slugger. Besides that hit, he was only 1 for 11.

5) C. ... yes, he did."
In terms of displaying a lack of enthusiasm when calling an exciting

Quiz begins on page 60

game, McCarver is surpassed in dullness only by his partner Joe Buck.

6) D. Derek Lowe

Pitching in extra-inning relief, Lowe won Game 3 of the Anaheim series. He then started and won Game 7 of the ALCS and Game 4 of the World Series, pitching a total of 13 innings and allowing only 1 run in those two games. Frustrated by being left out of the starting rotation in the postseason, his availability in key spots enabled him to become a postseason hero.

7) B. Tony Clark

The tying run was on base and Clark could have won the series for the Yankees with a home run, but instead he waved helplessly at a fastball high and away to end the game.

8) E. Pedro Martinez

Given Pedro's reputation as a "headhunter" on the mound, perhaps some fans thought it appropriate that he take one off the melon in one of his last acts as a Red Sox player.

9) E. Curtis Leskanic

Leskanic came into a two-out, bases-loaded jam in the top of the 11th inning and got Bernie Williams out on a fly to center. He then pitched a scoreless top of the 12th, setting up Big Papi's game-ending two-run blast in the bottom of the inning.

10) A. Kevin Millar

Millar didn't have too many memorable moments in the postseason, and an early two-run homer in an eventual 9-3 blowout certainly isn't all that memorable. Those watching closely, however, will always remember his walk in the 9th inning of Game 4 in the ALCS that represented the tying run and turned the series around.

Quiz begins on page 60

11) D. Yankees Stink
While all five headlines are delightful and appropriate, it was only "Yankees Stink" that the scribes from Gotham chose not to use to commemorate the Yankees historic collapse.

12) B. 8
Yes, the Red Sox committed 4 errors in Game 1 and 4 errors in Game 2 and still managed to win both games. Manny Ramirez made 2 errors in Game 1 and Bill Mueller made 3 in Game 2.

13) B. Mark Bellhorn
The diminutive second baseman hit a game-winning three-run homer in Game 6 of the ALCS, another solo shot in ALCS Game 7, and a game-winning two-run homer in Game 1 of the World Series. In the 2004 postseason, the Red Sox were truly Saved by the Bellhorn.

14) E. Gary Sheffield
While Sheffield was horrific at 1-17, his mates weren't much better: A-Rod was 2-17, Jeter was 4-19, and Posada was 4-17.

15) E. The Pesky Pole
Bellhorn's game-winner capped off the scoring in a wild 11-9 game. In the prior game at Yankee Stadium, Bellhorn also hit a homer off the right field foul pole.

16) C. Bill Mueller
The quiet, hard-working professional got the job done and came through with one of the biggest hits in team history.

17) B. Tim Wakefield
It was certainly appropriate that the honor of starting the first World Series game to be played in Fenway Park in 18 years go to Wakefield,

Quiz begins on page 60

the senior member of the team with 10 years of service at the time, and someone renowned for his hard work and selfless attitude.

18) B. 1

Foulke was stellar in the World Series, pitching a total of 5 innings, giving up only one run, while allowing four hits and one walk with 8 strikeouts. He recorded the last out of each of the four games, but only 1 save. He was the winning pitcher in Game 1, and Games 2 and 3 were non-save situations. His only save came in Game 4.

19) E. Dr. Bill Morgan

One of the great unsung heroes in Red Sox history, team doctor Bill Morgan practiced his experimental procedure on human cadaver legs before inserting several sutures into Schilling's ankle to help keep the tendon in place.

20) E. 3

Renteria wore the same number as Babe Ruth. The Curse of the Bambino, if you believe in it, was finally broken.

Quiz begins on page 60

Understanding the
Grandstand Section Diagrams

Detail of Section 12 Seating Diagram
Bold numbers running vertically are row numbers
Numbers in boxes running horizontally are seat numbers

The seating diagrams in this book are intended to help you identify the seats in Grandstand sections that have **a pole impeding your view of home plate, the pitcher's mound, or both.** Grandstand section seats are the only seats in the park that have poles between the fans and the field.

As you can see in this detail from Section 12, the shaded areas cover seats that have a pole between them and either home plate or the pitcher's mound. In this case, the shaded area on the right has a home plate obstruction, and the shaded area on the left has a pitcher's mound obstruction.

So, if you sit in Section 12, Row 7, Seat 7 you will have difficulty seeing home plate without having to move forward, backward, or side to side. Similarly, if you sit in Row 4, Seat 6 you will have difficulty seeing the pitcher's mound.

Many seat numbers are partially shaded. This means that the pole issues affecting that seat are not as intrusive as seats that are completely shaded. If you're not sure if a seat will have any pole issues by looking at the diagrams, it would be a good idea to pick seats that are at least 2 completely non-shaded seats away from the obstructed area.

Generally, the further back you are in a section, the less of a problem the pole will be for your view. The closer you are to a pole, the bigger it looks.

Section 1

Outfield Grandstand
Face Value of tickets is $30

Section 1 is in right field behind Right
Field Box 87.

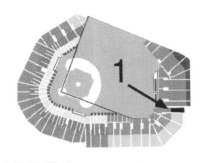

Section 1 borders the bleacher seats,
and the main difference between
sitting in Section 1 or rows 15–30 of
Bleacher Section 43 is that Section 1
is covered by a roof in case it rains. With only 8 seats in each row, it does
make the seats feel less congested than most other sections and you have
easier access to the aisle. Also, unlike many of the other Outfield
Grandstand sections, these seats face home plate, and not left field.

There is a pole near row 1, seat 1 that affects that seat and one or two others
in each row running diagonally up to row 17, seat 5.

The view from the center of Section 1

Section 1

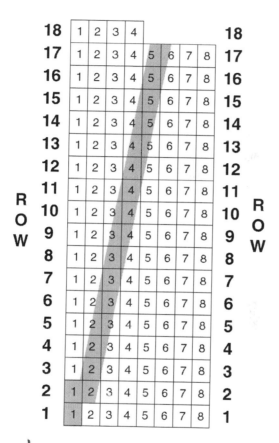

= View of home plate or pitcher's mound is obstructed

home plate

Section 2

Outfield Grandstand
Face Value of tickets is $30

Section 2 is in right field behind Right
Field Box 88.

Section 2 is a large section in right
field that is far from home plate.
Unlike many of the other Outfield
Grandstand sections, these seats face home plate, and not left field.

If you are facing the field, pole issues are limited to some seats on the left
side of the section. Any seat numbered 1 through 18 is free from poles.

The view from the center of Section 2

Section 2

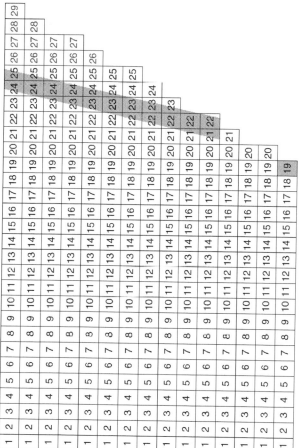

= View of home plate or pitcher's mound is obstructed

home plate

Section 3

Outfield Grandstand
Face Value of tickets is $30

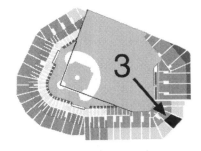

Section 3 is in right field behind Right
Field Box 89.

Section 3 is a large section directly
down the right field line that is far
from home plate. Unlike many of the
other Outfield Grandstand sections, these seats face the infield, and not
left field.

If you are facing the field, pole issues are limited to some seats on the left
side of the section. Beginning in row 4, seat 25, the obstruction affects some
seats up to row 15, seat 25. All the seats in rows 1 through 3 are safe from
poles, as well as any seats numbered 1 through 22 in the entire section.

The view from the center of Section 3

Section 3

ROW (top labels): 15 14 13 12 11 10 9 8 7 6 5 4 3 2 1

15	14	13	12	11	10	9	8	7	6	5	4	3	2	1
33	33	32	31	31	30	29	29	28	27	27	26	25	24	24
32	32	31	30	30	29	28	28	27	26	26	25	24	23	23
31	31	30	29	29	28	27	27	26	25	25	24	23	22	22
30	30	29	28	28	27	26	26	25	24	24	23	22	21	21
29	29	28	27	27	26	25	25	24	23	23	22	21	20	20
28	28	27	26	26	25	24	24	23	22	22	21	20	19	19
27	27	26	25	25	24	23	23	22	21	21	20	19	18	18
26	26	25	24	24	23	22	22	21	20	20	19	18	17	17
25	25	24	23	23	22	21	21	20	19	19	18	17	16	16
24	24	23	22	22	21	20	20	19	18	18	17	16	15	15
23	23	22	21	21	20	19	19	18	17	17	16	15	14	14
22	22	21	20	20	19	18	18	17	16	16	15	14	13	13
21	21	20	19	19	18	17	17	16	15	15	14	13	12	12
20	20	19	18	18	17	16	16	15	14	14	13	12	11	11
19	19	18	17	17	16	15	15	14	13	13	12	11	10	10
18	18	17	16	16	15	14	14	13	12	12	11	10	9	9
17	17	16	15	15	14	13	13	12	11	11	10	9	8	8
16	16	15	14	14	13	12	12	11	10	10	9	8	7	7
15	15	14	13	13	12	11	11	10	9	9	8	7	6	6
14	14	13	12	12	11	10	10	9	8	8	7	6	5	5
13	13	12	11	11	10	9	9	8	7	7	6	5	4	4
12	12	11	10	10	9	8	8	7	6	6	5	4	3	3
11	11	10	9	9	8	7	7	6	5	5	4	3	2	2
10	10	9	8	8	7	6	6	5	4	4	3	2	1	1
9	9	8	7	7	6	5	5	4	3	3	2	1		
8	8	7	6	6	5	4	4	3	2	2	1			
7	7	6	5	5	4	3	3	2	1	1				
6	6	5	4	4	3	2	2	1						
5	5	4	3	3	2	1	1							
4	4	3	2	2	1									
3	3	2	1	1										
2	2	1												
1	1													

ROW (bottom labels): 15 14 13 12 11 10 9 8 7 6 5 4 3 2 1

→ home plate

= View of home plate or pitcher's mound is obstructed

Section 4

Outfield Grandstand
Face Value of tickets is $30

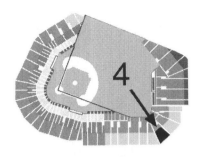

Section 4 is in right field behind Right
Field Box 90.

Tucked away in the right field corner,
seats in this section are very far from
home plate and they face the left field
foul pole, rather than the infield, which causes you to have to look to the
left to see the action. Although they are fairly priced at $30, these are not
very good seats.

There is a pole that affects seats 26 and 27 in the second row, and the
obstruction runs diagonally up through the section to seats 19 and 20 in
row 17.

The view from the center of Section 4

Section 4

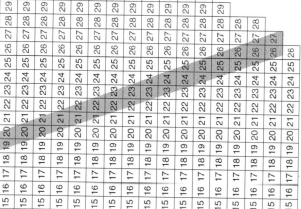

= View of home plate or pitcher's mound is obstructed

home plate

Section 5

Outfield Grandstand
Face Value of tickets is $30

Section 5 is in right field behind Right
Field Box 91.

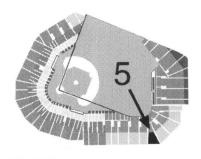

Tucked away in the right field corner,
seats in this section are very far from
home plate and they face the Green
Monster, rather than the infield,
which causes you to have to look to the left to see the action. Although they
are fairly priced at $30, these are some of the worst seats in Fenway.

There is a pole obstruction that runs diagonally across the section from the
last few seats in row 3 to the first few seats in row 9. All seats in rows 1, 2,
and 10-17 are free from pole issues.

The view from the center of Section 5

Section 5

ROW 17 16 15 14 13 12 11 10 9 8 7 6 5 4 3 2 1

home plate

 = View of home plate or pitcher's mound is obstructed

ROW 17 16 15 14 13 12 11 10 9 8 7 6 5 4 3 2 1

Section 6

Outfield Grandstand
Face Value of tickets is $30

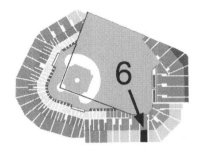

Section 6 is in right field behind Right
Field Box 92.

Tucked away in the right field corner,
seats in this section are far from home
plate and they face center field, rather
than the infield, which causes you to have to look to the left to see the
action. Compared to most other sections in the park, these are not very
good seats.

There is a pole obstruction that runs from the last few seats in rows 4 and 5
diagonally across the section to the first seat in row 12. All seats in rows 1-3
and 13-17 are free from pole issues.

The view from the center of Section 6

Section 6

ROW	1	2	3	4	5	6	7	8	9	10	11	12	13	14	15	16	17	18	19	20	21	ROW
17	1	2	3	4	5	6	7	8	9	10	11	12	13	14	15	16	17	18	19	20	21	**17**
16	1	2	3	4	5	6	7	8	9	10	11	12	13	14	15	16	17	18	19	20	21	**16**
15	1	2	3	4	5	6	7	8	9	10	11	12	13	14	15	16	17	18	19	20	21	**15**
14	1	2	3	4	5	6	7	8	9	10	11	12	13	14	15	16	17	18	19	20	21	**14**
13	1	2	3	4	5	6	7	8	9	10	11	12	13	14	15	16	17	18	19	20	21	**13**
12	1	2	3	4	5	6	7	8	9	10	11	12	13	14	15	16	17	18	19	20	21	**12**
11	1	2	3	4	5	6	7	8	9	10	11	12	13	14	15	16	17	18	19	20	21	**11**
10	1	2	3	4	5	6	7	8	9	10	11	12	13	14	15	16	17	18	19	20	21	**10**
9	1	2	3	4	5	6	7	8	9	10	11	12	13	14	15	16	17	18	19	20	21	**9**
8	1	2	3	4	5	6	7	8	9	10	11	12	13	14	15	16	17	18	19	20	21	**8**
7	1	2	3	4	5	6	7	8	9	10	11	12	13	14	15	16	17	18	19	20	21	**7**
6	1	2	3	4	5	6	7	8	9	10	11	12	13	14	15	16	17	18	19	20	21	**6**
5	1	2	3	4	5	6	7	8	9	10	11	12	13	14	15	16	17	18	19	20	21	**5**
4	1	2	3	4	5	6	7	8	9	10	11	12	13	14	15	16	17	18	19	20	21	**4**
3	1	2	3	4	5	6	7	8	9	10	11	12	13	14	15	16	17	18	19	20	21	**3**
2	1	2	3	4	5	6	7	8	9	10	11	12	13	14	15	16	17	18	19	20	21	**2**
1	1	2	3	4	5	6	7	8	9	10	11	12	13	14	15	16	17	18	19	20	21	**1**

= View of home plate or pitcher's mound is obstructed

home plate

Section 7

Outfield Grandstand
Face Value of tickets is $30

Section 7 is in right field behind Right
Field Box 93.

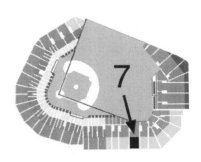

Located down the right field line past
the foul pole, seats in this section are
far from home plate and they face left
field, rather than the infield, which
causes you to have to look to the left to see the action. Compared to most
other sections in the park, these are not very good seats.

There are two pole obstructions in this section, one that affects the first few
rows in the lower-numbered seats, and one that runs diagonally across the
middle rows.

The view from the center of Section 7

Section 7

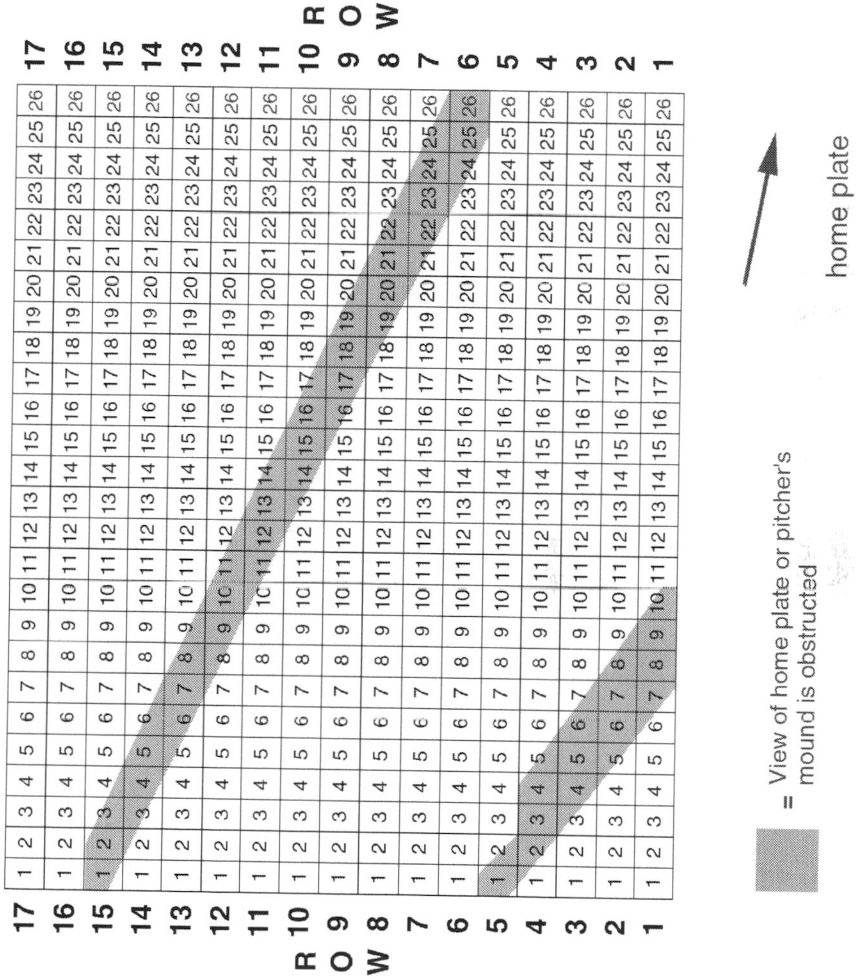

ROW

home plate

= View of home plate or pitcher's mound is obstructed

Section 8

Outfield Grandstand
Face Value of tickets is $30

Section 8 is in right field behind Right
Field Box 94.

Located down the right field line near
the foul pole, seats in this section face
left field, rather than the infield, which
causes you to have to look to the left
to see the action.

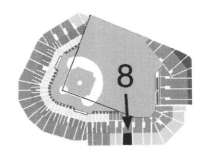

There are two pole obstructions in this section, one that affects the first few
rows in the lower-numbered seats, and one that runs diagonally across rows
7 through 17.

The view from the center of Section 8

Section 8

home plate

= View of home plate or pitcher's
mound is obstructed

Section 9

Outfield Grandstand
Face Value of tickets is $30

Section 9 is in right field behind Right
Field Box 95.

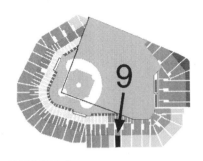

Located down the right field line,
seats in this section face left field,
rather than the infield, which causes
you to have to look to the left to see
the action.

There are two pole obstructions in this section, one that affects some seats
in rows 1 through 7, and another that affects some seats in rows 14 through
17. All seats in rows 8 through 13 are free from pole issues.

The view from the center of Section 9

Section 9

ROW																		ROW
17	1	2	3	4	5	6	7	8	9	10	11	12	13	14	15	16	**17**
16	1	2	3	4	5	6	7	8	9	10	11	12	13	14	15	16	**16**
15	1	2	3	4	5	6	7	8	9	10	11	12	13	14	15	16	**15**
14	1	2	3	4	5	6	7	8	9	10	11	12	13	14	15	16	**14**
13	1	2	3	4	5	6	7	8	9	10	11	12	13	14	15	16	**13**
12	1	2	3	4	5	6	7	8	9	10	11	12	13	14	15	16	**12**
11	1	2	3	4	5	6	7	8	9	10	11	12	13	14	15	16	**11**
10	1	2	3	4	5	6	7	8	9	10	11	12	13	14	15	16	**10**
9	1	2	3	4	5	6	7	8	9	10	11	12	13	14	15	16	**9**
8	1	2	3	4	5	6	7	8	9	10	11	12	13	14	15	16	**8**
7	1	2	3	4	5	6	7	8	9	10	11	12	13	14	15	16	**7**
6	1	2	3	4	5	6	7	8	9	10	11	12	13	14	15	16	**6**
5	1	2	3	4	5	6	7	8	9	10	11	12	13	14	15	16	**5**
4	1	2	3	4	5	6	7	8	9	10	11	12	13	14	15	16	**4**
3	1	2	3	4	5	6	7	8	9	10	11	12	13	14	15	16	**3**
2	1	2	3	4	5	6	7	8	9	10	11	12	13	14	15	16	**2**
1	1	2	3	4	5	6	7	8	9	10	11	12	13	14	15	16	**1**

= View of home plate or pitcher's mound is obstructed

home plate

Section 10

Outfield Grandstand
Face Value of tickets is $30

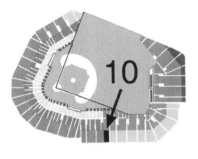

Section 10 is in right field behind
Right Field Box 97.

Located down the right field line, this
section is closer to the infield than
any other leftfield grandstand section.
The seats in neighboring Section 11 have a face value of $50.

There is one obstruction in this section, beginning with the last seat in row
5 moving diagonally to the first seat in row 11. All seats in rows 1-4 and 12-
17 are free from poles.

The view from the center of Section 10

Section 10

ROW														ROW
17	1	2	3	4	5	6	7	8	9	10	11	12	13	17
16	1	2	3	4	5	6	7	8	9	10	11	12	13	16
15	1	2	3	4	5	6	7	8	9	10	11	12	13	15
14	1	2	3	4	5	6	7	8	9	10	11	12	13	14
13	1	2	3	4	5	6	7	8	9	10	11	12	13	13
12	1	2	3	4	5	6	7	8	9	10	11	12	13	12
11	1	2	3	4	5	6	7	8	9	10	11	12	13	11
10	1	2	3	4	5	6	7	8	9	10	11	12	13	10
9	1	2	3	4	5	6	7	8	9	10	11	12	13	9
8	1	2	3	4	5	6	7	8	9	10	11	12	13	8
7	1	2	3	4	5	6	7	8	9	10	11	12	13	7
6	1	2	3	4	5	6	7	8	9	10	11	12	13	6
5	1	2	3	4	5	6	7	8	9	10	11	12	13	5
4	1	2	3	4	5	6	7	8	9	10	11	12	13	4
3	1	2	3	4	5	6	7	8	9	10	11	12	13	3
2	1	2	3	4	5	6	7	8	9	10	11	12	13	2
1	1	2	3	4	5	6	7	8	9	10	11	12	13	1

= View of home plate or pitcher's mound is obstructed

home plate

Section 11

Infield Grandstand
Face Value of tickets is $52

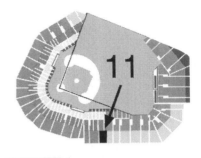

Section 11 is down the right field line
behind Loge Box sections 98-100
and Field Box sections 9-10.

Section 11 borders Outfield
Grandstand Section 10, where
tickets have a face value of $30. This means that Section 11 is farther away
from home plate than any other Infield Grandstand section on the first base
side, and seats in Section 11 are much closer to the Pesky Pole than they
are to first base.

Pole issues in Section 11 are fairly mild. If you are seated anywhere in the
middle of the section you will have a clear view.

The view from the center of Section 11

Section 11

ROW																					ROW
17	1	2	3	4	5	6	7	8	9	10	11	12	13	14	15	16	17	18	19	20	**17**
16	1	2	3	4	5	6	7	8	9	10	11	12	13	14	15	16	17	18	19	20	**16**
15	1	2	3	4	5	6	7	8	9	10	11	12	13	14	15	16	17	18	19	20	**15**
14	1	2	3	4	5	6	7	8	9	10	11	12	13	14	15	16	17	18	19	20	**14**
13	1	2	3	4	5	6	7	8	9	10	11	12	13	14	15	16	17	18	19	20	**13**
12	1	2	3	4	5	6	7	8	9	10	11	12	13	14	15	16	17	18	19	20	**12**
11	1	2	3	4	5	6	7	8	9	10	11	12	13	14	15	16	17	18	19	20	**11**
10	1	2	3	4	5	6	7	8	9	10	11	12	13	14	15	16	17	18	19	20	**10**
9	1	2	3	4	5	6	7	8	9	10	11	12	13	14	15	16	17	18	19	20	**9**
8	1	2	3	4	5	6	7	8	9	10	11	12	13	14	15	16	17	18	19	20	**8**
7	1	2	3	4	5	6	7	8	9	10	11	12	13	14	15	16	17	18	19	20	**7**
6	1	2	3	4	5	6	7	8	9	10	11	12	13	14	15	16	17	18	19	20	**6**
5	1	2	3	4	5	6	7	8	9	10	11	12	13	14	15	16	17	18	19	20	**5**
4	1	2	3	4	5	6	7	8	9	10	11	12	13	14	15	16	17	18	19	20	**4**
3	1	2	3	4	5	6	7	8	9	10	11	12	13	14	15	16	17	18	19	20	**3**
2	1	2	3	4	5	6	7	8	9	10	11	12	13	14	15	16	17	18	19	20	**2**
1	1	2	3	4	5	6	7	8	9	10	11	12	13	14	15	16	17	18	19	20	**1**

= View of home plate or pitcher's mound is obstructed

home plate

93

Section 12

Infield Grandstand
Face Value of tickets is $52

Section 12 is down the right field line
behind Loge Box sections 101-104 and
Field Box sections 11-15.

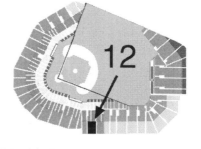

Pole issues in Section 12 are confined
to the right side of the section if you are
facing the field. Any seat with a number of 15 or higher is safe from poles.

The view from the center of Section 12

Section 12

ROW																									ROW
17	1	2	3	4	5	6	7	8	9	10	11	12	13	14	15	16	17	18	19	20	21	22	23	24		**17**
16	1	2	3	4	5	6	7	8	9	10	11	12	13	14	15	16	17	18	19	20	21	22	23	24	25	**16**
15	1	2	3	4	5	6	7	8	9	10	11	12	13	14	15	16	17	18	19	20	21	22	23	24	25	**15**
14	1	2	3	4	5	6	7	8	9	10	11	12	13	14	15	16	17	18	19	20	21	22	23	24	25	**14**
13	1	2	3	4	5	6	7	8	9	10	11	12	13	14	15	16	17	18	19	20	21	22	23	24	25	**13**
12	1	2	3	4	5	6	7	8	9	10	11	12	13	14	15	16	17	18	19	20	21	22	23	24	25	**12**
11	1	2	3	4	5	6	7	8	9	10	11	12	13	14	15	16	17	18	19	20	21	22	23	24	25	**11**
10	1	2	3	4	5	6	7	8	9	10	11	12	13	14	15	16	17	18	19	20	21	22	23	24	25	**10**
9	1	2	3	4	5	6	7	8	9	10	11	12	13	14	15	16	17	18	19	20	21	22	23	24	25	**9**
8	1	2	3	4	5	6	7	8	9	10	11	12	13	14	15	16	17	18	19	20	21	22	23	24	25	**8**
7	1	2	3	4	5	6	7	8	9	10	11	12	13	14	15	16	17	18	19	20	21	22	23	24	25	**7**
6	1	2	3	4	5	6	7	8	9	10	11	12	13	14	15	16	17	18	19	20	21	22	23	24	25	**6**
5	1	2	3	4	5	6	7	8	9	10	11	12	13	14	15	16	17	18	19	20	21	22	23	24	25	**5**
4	1	2	3	4	5	6	7	8	9	10	11	12	13	14	15	16	17	18	19	20	21	22	23	24	25	**4**
3	1	2	3	4	5	6	7	8	9	10	11	12	13	14	15	16	17	18	19	20	21	22	23	24	25	**3**
2	1	2	3	4	5	6	7	8	9	10	11	12	13	14	15	16	17	18	19	20	21	22	23	24	25	**2**
1	1	2	3	4	5	6	7	8	9	10	11	12	13	14	15	16	17	18	19	20	21	22	23	24	25	**1**

 = View of home plate or pitcher's mound is obstructed

home plate

Section 13

Infield Grandstand
Face Value of tickets is $52

Section 13 is down the first base line
behind Loge Box section 105 and Field
Box section 19.

Of all 33 Grandstand sections, 13 is
one of the two smallest. Only 12 seats
wide on the bottom, it gradually narrows to 6 seats in the last 4 rows.

Pole issues in Section 13 run right down the middle of the section. If you
are sitting in the middle of the section you will see a pole between home
plate and the pitcher's mound. If you are sitting on the left or right side of
the section, there is a good chance you will have a problem with a pole.

The view from the center of Section 13

Section 13

ROW													ROW
16	1	2	3	4	5	6							16
15	1	2	3	4	5	6							15
14	1	2	3	4	5	6							14
13	1	2	3	4	5	6							13
12	1	2	3	4	5	6	7						12
11	1	2	3	4	5	6	7	8					11
10	1	2	3	4	5	6	7	8	9	10			10
9	1	2	3	4	5	6	7	8	9	10	11		9
8	1	2	3	4	5	6	7	8	9	10	11		8
7	1	2	3	4	5	6	7	8	9	10	11		7
6	1	2	3	4	5	6	7	8	9	10	11	12	6
5	1	2	3	4	5	6	7	8	9	10	11	12	5
4	1	2	3	4	5	6	7	8	9	10	11	12	4
3	1	2	3	4	5	6	7	8	9	10	11	12	3
2	1	2	3	4	5	6	7	8	9	10	11	12	2
1	1	2	3	4	5	6	7	8	9	10	11	12	1

= View of home plate or pitcher's mound is obstructed

home plate

Section 14

Infield Grandstand
Face Value of tickets is $52

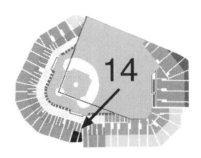

Section 14 is down the first base line
behind Loge Boxes 106-110 and Field
Boxes 20-23.

It is located behind first base and the
home dugout, and an aisle runs down
the middle of the section. Because of
the aisle you may have seats that are numbered consecutively but are
actually across the aisle from one another.

Pole issues in Section 14 are limited to the left side of the section if you are
facing the field. If you are seated anywhere to the right of the aisle you will
have a clear view.

The view from the center of Section 14

Section 14

home plate →

ROW

15	14	13	12	11	10	9	8	7	6	5	4	3	2	1
16	23	26	29	29	29	28	28	28	27	27	26	26	25	24
15	22	25	28	28	28	27	27	27	26	26	25	25	24	23
14	21	24	27	27	27	26	26	26	25	25	24	24	23	22
13	20	23	26	26	26	25	25	25	24	24	23	23	22	21
12	19	22	25	25	25	24	24	24	23	23	22	22	21	20
11	18	21	24	24	24	23	23	23	22	22	21	21	20	19
10	17	20	23	23	23	22	22	22	21	21	20	20	19	18
9	16	19	22	22	22	21	21	21	20	20	19	19	18	17
8	15	18	21	21	21	20	20	20	19	19	18	18	17	16
7	14	17	20	20	20	19	19	19	18	18	17	17	16	15
6	13	16	19	19	19	18	18	18	17	17	16	16	15	14
5	12	15	18	18	18	17	17	17	16	16	15	15	14	13
4	11	14	17	17	17	16	16	16	15	15	14	14	13	12
3	10	13	16	16	16	15	15	15	14	14	13	13	12	11
2	9	12	15	15	15	14	14	14	13	13	12	12	11	10

AISLE

15	14	13	12	11	10	9	8	7	6	5	4	3	2	1
1	8	11	14	14	14	13	13	13	12	12	11	11	10	9
	7	10	13	13	13	12	12	12	11	11	10	10	9	8
	6	9	12	12	12	11	11	11	10	10	9	9	8	7
	5	8	11	11	11	10	10	10	9	9	8	8	7	6
	4	7	10	10	10	9	9	9	8	8	7	7	6	5
	3	6	9	9	9	8	8	8	7	7	6	6	5	4
	2	5	8	8	8	7	7	7	6	6	5	5	4	3
	1	4	7	7	7	6	6	6	5	5	4	4	3	2
		3	6	6	6	5	5	5	4	4	3	3	2	1
		2	5	5	5	4	4	4	3	3	2	2	1	
		1	4	4	4	3	3	3	2	2	1	1		
			3	3	3	2	2	2	1	1				
			2	2	2	1	1	1						
			1	1	1									

ROW

= View of home plate or pitcher's mound is obstructed

Section 15

Infield Grandstand
Face Value of tickets is $52

Section 15 is down the first base line
behind Loge Boxes 111-114 and Field
Boxes 24-28.

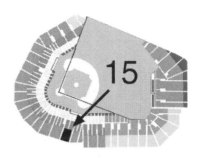

It is located in between home plate
and first base and provides an
excellent view of the field and the
entire park.

Pole issues are limited to the left side of the section if you are facing the
field.

The view from the center of Section 15

Section 15

ROW		1	2	3	4	5	6	7	8	9	10	11	12	13	14	15	16	17	18	19	20	21	22	23	24		ROW
19		1	2	3	4	5	6	7	8	9	10	11	12	13	14	15	16	17	18	19	20	21	22	23	24	19	
18		1	2	3	4	5	6	7	8	9	10	11	12	13	14	15	16	17	18	19	20	21	22	23	24	18	
17		1	2	3	4	5	6	7	8	9	10	11	12	13	14	15	16	17	18	19	20	21	22	23	24	17	
16			1	2	3	4	5	6	7	8	9	10	11	12	13	14	15	16	17	18	19	20	21	22	23	16	
15			1	2	3	4	5	6	7	8	9	10	11	12	13	14	15	16	17	18	19	20	21	22	23	15	
14		1	2	3	4	5	6	7	8	9	10	11	12	13	14	15	16	17	18	19	20	21	22	23	24	14	
13		1	2	3	4	5	6	7	8	9	10	11	12	13	14	15	16	17	18	19	20	21	22	23	24	13	
12		1	2	3	4	5	6	7	8	9	10	11	12	13	14	15	16	17	18	19	20	21	22	23	24	12	
11		1	2	3	4	5	6	7	8	9	10	11	12	13	14	15	16	17	18	19	20	21	22	23	24	11	
10		1	2	3	4	5	6	7	8	9	10	11	12	13	14	15	16	17	18	19	20	21	22	23	24	10	
9		1	2	3	4	5	6	7	8	9	10	11	12	13	14	15	16	17	18	19	20	21	22	23	24	9	
8		1	2	3	4	5	6	7	8	9	10	11	12	13	14	15	16	17	18	19	20	21	22	23	24	8	
7		1	2	3	4	5	6	7	8	9	10	11	12	13	14	15	16	17	18	19	20	21	22	23	24	7	
6		1	2	3	4	5	6	7	8	9	10	11	12	13	14	15	16	17	18	19	20	21	22	23	24	6	
5		1	2	3	4	5	6	7	8	9	10	11	12	13	14	15	16	17	18	19	20	21	22	23	24	5	
4		1	2	3	4	5	6	7	8	9	10	11	12	13	14	15	16	17	18	19	20	21	22	23	24	4	
3		1	2	3	4	5	6	7	8	9	10	11	12	13	14	15	16	17	18	19	20	21	22	23	24	3	
2		1	2	3	4	5	6	7	8	9	10	11	12	13	14	15	16	17	18	19	20	21	22	23	24	2	
1			1	2	3	4	5	6	7	8	9	10	11	12	13	14	15	16	17	18	19	20	21	22	23	1	

 = View of home plate or pitcher's mound is obstructed

home plate

Section 16

Infield Grandstand
Face Value of tickets is $52

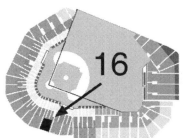

Section 16 is on the first base line behind Loge Boxes 115-118 and Field Boxes 29-32.

It is located in between home plate and first base and provides an excellent view of the field and the entire park.

Pole issues are limited to the left side of the section if you are facing the field.

The view from the center of Section 16

Section 16

ROW	Seats	ROW
19	1 2 3 4 5 6 7 8 9 10 11 12 13 14 15 16 17 18 19 20 21 **22** 23 24	19
18	1 2 3 4 5 6 7 8 9 10 11 12 13 14 15 16 17 18 19 20 21 **22** 23 24	18
17	1 2 3 4 5 6 7 8 9 10 11 12 13 14 15 16 17 18 19 20 21 **22** 23 24	17
16	1 2 3 4 5 6 7 8 9 10 11 12 13 14 15 16 17 18 19 20 21 22 23 **24** 25 26	16
15	1 2 3 4 5 6 7 8 9 10 11 12 13 14 15 16 17 18 19 20 21 22 23 **24** 25 26	15
14	1 2 3 4 5 6 7 8 9 10 11 12 13 14 15 16 17 18 19 20 21 22 23 **24** 25 26	14
13	1 2 3 4 5 6 7 8 9 10 11 12 13 14 15 16 17 18 19 20 21 22 23 **24** 25 26	13
12	1 2 3 4 5 6 7 8 9 10 11 12 13 14 15 16 17 18 19 20 21 22 23 **24** 25 26	12
11	1 2 3 4 5 6 7 8 9 10 11 12 13 14 15 16 17 18 19 20 21 22 23 **24 25** 26	11
10	1 2 3 4 5 6 7 8 9 10 11 12 13 14 15 16 17 18 19 20 21 22 23 **24 25** 26	10
9	1 2 3 4 5 6 7 8 9 10 11 12 13 14 15 16 17 18 19 20 21 22 23 **24 25 26**	9
8	1 2 3 4 5 6 7 8 9 10 11 12 13 14 15 16 17 18 19 20 21 22 23 **24 25 26**	8
7	1 2 3 4 5 6 7 8 9 10 11 12 13 14 15 16 17 18 19 20 21 22 23 **24 25 26**	7
6	1 2 3 4 5 6 7 8 9 10 11 12 13 14 15 16 17 18 19 20 21 22 23 **24 25 26**	6
5	1 2 3 4 5 6 7 8 9 10 11 12 13 14 15 16 17 18 19 20 21 22 23 **24 25 26**	5
4	1 2 3 4 5 6 7 8 9 10 11 12 13 14 15 16 17 18 19 20 21 22 23 **24 25 26**	4
3	1 2 3 4 5 6 7 8 9 10 11 12 13 14 15 16 17 18 19 20 21 22 23 **24 25 26**	3
2	1 2 3 4 5 6 7 8 9 10 11 12 13 14 15 16 17 18 19 20 21 22 23 **24 25 26**	2
1	1 2 3 4 5 6 7 8 9 10 11 12 13 14 15 16 17 18 19 20 21 22 23 24 25 26	1

 = View of home plate or pitcher's mound is obstructed

home plate

Section 17

Infield Grandstand
Face Value of tickets is $52

Section 17 is near the Sox on deck
circle behind Loge Boxes 119-122
and Field Boxes 33-36.

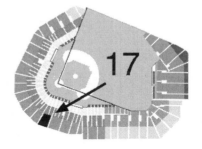

The view from the center of the
section is straight down the third base
line. It is one of the better sections to sit in, because there are very few seats
with pole issues and there are also no home plate screen issues.

Pole issues are limited to a few seats on the right side of the section if you
are facing the field.

The view from the center of Section 17

Section 17

ROW

18 15 14 13 12 11 10 9 8 7 6 5 4 3 2 1

Wheelchair Seating Row
(Installed prior to 2009 season)

ROW	Seats
18	1
15	1 2 3 4 5 6 7 8 9 10 11 12 13 14 15 16 17 18 19 20 21 22 23 24 25 26 27 28 29
14	2 3 4 5 6 7 8 9 10 11 12 13 14 15 16 17 18 19 20 21 22 23 24 25 26 27 28
13	1 2 3 4 5 6 7 8 9 10 11 12 13 14 15 16 17 18 19 20 21 22 23 24 25 26 27 28
12	1 2 3 4 5 6 7 8 9 10 11 12 13 14 15 16 17 18 19 20 21 22 23 24 25 26 27 28
11	1 2 3 4 5 6 7 8 9 10 11 12 13 14 15 16 17 18 19 20 21 22 23 24 25 26 27
10	1 2 3 4 5 6 7 8 9 10 11 12 13 14 15 16 17 18 19 20 21 22 23 24 25 26 27
9	1 2 3 4 5 6 7 8 9 10 11 12 13 14 15 16 17 18 19 20 21 22 23 24 25 26 27
8	1 2 3 4 5 6 7 8 9 10 11 12 13 14 15 16 17 18 19 20 21 22 23 24 25 26
7	1 2 3 4 5 6 7 8 9 10 11 12 13 14 15 16 17 18 19 20 21 22 23 24 25 26
6	1 2 3 4 5 6 7 8 9 10 11 12 13 14 15 16 17 18 19 20 21 22 23 24 25
5	1 2 3 4 5 6 7 8 9 10 11 12 13 14 15 16 17 18 19 20 21 22 23 24 25
4	1 2 3 4 5 6 7 8 9 10 11 12 13 14 15 16 17 18 19 20 21 22 23 24 25
3	1 2 3 4 5 6 7 8 9 10 11 12 13 14 15 16 17 18 19 20 21 22 23 24
2	1 2 3 4 5 6 7 8 9 10 11 12 13 14 15 16 17 18 19 20 21 22 23 24
1	1 2 3 4 5 6 7 8 9 10 11 12 13 14 15 16 17 18 19 20 21 22 23 24

ROW

18 15 14 13 12 11 10 9 8 7 6 5 4 3 2 1

= View of home plate or pitcher's mound is obstructed

home plate

Section 18

Infield Grandstand
Face Value of tickets is $52

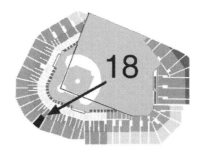

Section 18 is near home plate behind
Loge Boxes 123-125 and Field Boxes
38-40.

The vast majority of the seats in this
section are very good, as they can
rightly be described as being "behind home plate." Some of the seats on
the left side of the section facing the field have the home plate foul ball
screen to look through, which can be a minor annoyance.

There is a pole that obstructs the view of seats 4, 5, 6, or 7 in most of the
rows.

The view from the center of Section 18

Section 18

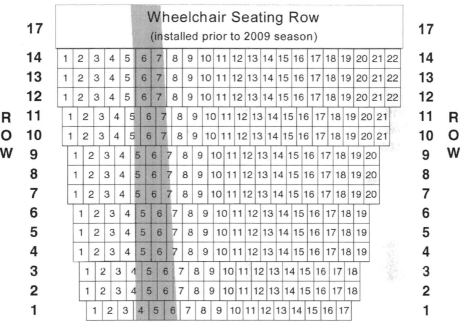

ROW		
17	Wheelchair Seating Row (installed prior to 2009 season)	17
14	1 2 3 4 5 6 7 8 9 10 11 12 13 14 15 16 17 18 19 20 21 22	14
13	1 2 3 4 5 6 7 8 9 10 11 12 13 14 15 16 17 18 19 20 21 22	13
12	1 2 3 4 5 6 7 8 9 10 11 12 13 14 15 16 17 18 19 20 21 22	12
11	1 2 3 4 5 6 7 8 9 10 11 12 13 14 15 16 17 18 19 20 21	11
10	1 2 3 4 5 6 7 8 9 10 11 12 13 14 15 16 17 18 19 20 21	10
9	1 2 3 4 5 6 7 8 9 10 11 12 13 14 15 16 17 18 19 20	9
8	1 2 3 4 5 6 7 8 9 10 11 12 13 14 15 16 17 18 19 20	8
7	1 2 3 4 5 6 7 8 9 10 11 12 13 14 15 16 17 18 19 20	7
6	1 2 3 4 5 6 7 8 9 10 11 12 13 14 15 16 17 18 19	6
5	1 2 3 4 5 6 7 8 9 10 11 12 13 14 15 16 17 18 19	5
4	1 2 3 4 5 6 7 8 9 10 11 12 13 14 15 16 17 18 19	4
3	1 2 3 4 5 6 7 8 9 10 11 12 13 14 15 16 17 18	3
2	1 2 3 4 5 6 7 8 9 10 11 12 13 14 15 16 17 18	2
1	1 2 3 4 5 6 7 8 9 10 11 12 13 14 15 16 17	1

R O W — R O W

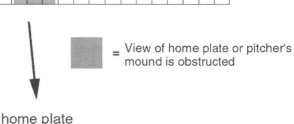

= View of home plate or pitcher's mound is obstructed

home plate

Section 19

Infield Grandstand
Face Value of tickets is $52

Section 19 is near home plate behind
Loge Boxes 126-128 and Field Boxes
40-41.

Section 19 is one of the best sections
in the entire park. Gloriously free
from any pole obstructions, it is behind home plate and offers a great view
of everything. The only minor annoyance could be looking through the
foul ball screen.

There are no pole issues in Section 19. Along with Section 21, it is one of
only two Grandstand Sections in the park completely unaffected by poles.

The view from the center of Section 19

Section 19

ROW																								ROW
18	1	2	3	4	5	6	7	8	9	10	11	12	13	14	15	16	17	18	19	20	21	22	23	**18**
17	1	2	3	4	5	6	7	8	9	10	11	12	13	14	15	16	17	18	19	20	21	22	23	**17**
16	1	2	3	4	5	6	7	8	9	10	11	12	13	14	15	16	17	18	19	20	21	22	23	**16**
15	1	2	3	4	5	6	7	8	9	10	11	12	13	14	15	16	17	18	19	20	21	22		**15**
14	1	2	3	4	5	6	7	8	9	10	11	12	13	14	15	16	17	18	19	20	21	22		**14**
13	1	2	3	4	5	6	7	8	9	10	11	12	13	14	15	16	17	18	19	20	21			**13**
12	1	2	3	4	5	6	7	8	9	10	11	12	13	14	15	16	17	18	19	20	21			**12**
11	1	2	3	4	5	6	7	8	9	10	11	12	13	14	15	16	17	18	19	20				**11**
10	1	2	3	4	5	6	7	8	9	10	11	12	13	14	15	16	17	18	19	20				**10**
9	1	2	3	4	5	6	7	8	9	10	11	12	13	14	15	16	17	18	19					**9**
8	1	2	3	4	5	6	7	8	9	10	11	12	13	14	15	16	17	18	19					**8**
7	1	2	3	4	5	6	7	8	9	10	11	12	13	14	15	16	17	18	19					**7**
6	1	2	3	4	5	6	7	8	9	10	11	12	13	14	15	16	17	18						**6**
5	1	2	3	4	5	6	7	8	9	10	11	12	13	14	15	16	17	18						**5**
4	1	2	3	4	5	6	7	8	9	10	11	12	13	14	15	16	17	18						**4**
3	1	2	3	4	5	6	7	8	9	10	11	12	13	14	15	16	17							**3**
2	1	2	3	4	5	6	7	8	9	10	11	12	13	14	15	16	17							**2**
1	1	2	3	4	5	6	7	8	9	10	11	12	13	14	15	16	17							**1**

There are no pole obstructions in Section 19

home plate

Section 20

Infield Grandstand
Face Value of tickets is $52

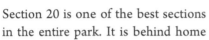

Section 20 is in back of home plate
behind Loge Boxes 129-130 and Field
Boxes 42-44.

Section 20 is one of the best sections
in the entire park. It is behind home
plate and offers a great view of everything. The only minor annoyance
could be looking through the foul ball screen.

Pole issues in Section 20 are limited to seats 1 and 2 in rows 3 through 18.
Any seat numbered 4 or higher is safe from poles.

The view from the center of Section 20

Section 20

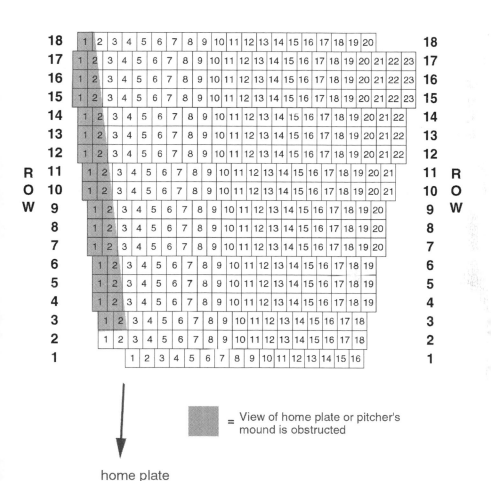

	R O W	home plate	R O W

= View of home plate or pitcher's mound is obstructed

Section 21

Infield Grandstand
Face Value of tickets is $52

Section 21 is near home plate behind
Loge Boxes 130-131 and Field Boxes
45-47.

Section 21 is one of the best sections
in the entire park. Gloriously free
from any pole obstructions, it is behind home plate and offers a great view
of everything. The only minor annoyance could be looking through the
foul ball screen.

There are no pole issues in Section 21. Along with Section 19, it is one of
only two Grandstand Sections in the park completely unaffected by poles.

The view from the center of Section 21

Section 21

ROW		Seats		ROW
16		1 2 3 4 5 6 7 8 9 10 11 12 13 14 15 16 17 18 19 20 21 22 23		16
15		1 2 3 4 5 6 7 8 9 10 11 12 13 14 15 16 17 18 19 20 21 22 23		15
14		1 2 3 4 5 6 7 8 9 10 11 12 13 14 15 16 17 18 19 20 21 22		14
13		1 2 3 4 5 6 7 8 9 10 11 12 13 14 15 16 17 18 19 20 21 22		13
12		1 2 3 4 5 6 7 8 9 10 11 12 13 14 15 16 17 18 19 20 21		12
11		1 2 3 4 5 6 7 8 9 10 11 12 13 14 15 16 17 18 19 20 21		11
10		1 2 3 4 5 6 7 8 9 10 11 12 13 14 15 16 17 18 19 20 21		10
9		1 2 3 4 5 6 7 8 9 10 11 12 13 14 15 16 17 18 19 20		9
8		1 2 3 4 5 6 7 8 9 10 11 12 13 14 15 16 17 18 19 20		8
7		1 2 3 4 5 6 7 8 9 10 11 12 13 14 15 16 17 18 19 20		7
6		1 2 3 4 5 6 7 8 9 10 11 12 13 14 15 16 17 18 19		6
5		1 2 3 4 5 6 7 8 9 10 11 12 13 14 15 16 17 18 19		5
4		1 2 3 4 5 6 7 8 9 10 11 12 13 14 15 16 17 18		4
3		1 2 3 4 5 6 7 8 9 10 11 12 13 14 15 16 17 18		3
2		1 2 3 4 5 6 7 8 9 10 11 12 13 14 15 16 17 18		2
1		1 2 3 4 5 6 7 8 9 10 11 12 13 14 15 16 17		1

There are no pole obstructions in Section 21

home plate

Section 22

Infield Grandstand
Face Value of tickets is $52

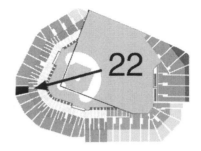

Section 22 is in back of home plate
behind Loge Boxes 132-134 and Field
Boxes 48-49.

Section 22 is one of the better
sections in the entire park. It is behind
home plate on the third base side and offers a great view of everything. The
only minor annoyance could be looking through the foul ball screen.

Pole issues in Section 22 are limited to seats 1 and, in come cases, 2 in rows
2 through 16. Any seat numbered 3 or higher is safe from poles.

The view from the center of Section 22

Section 22

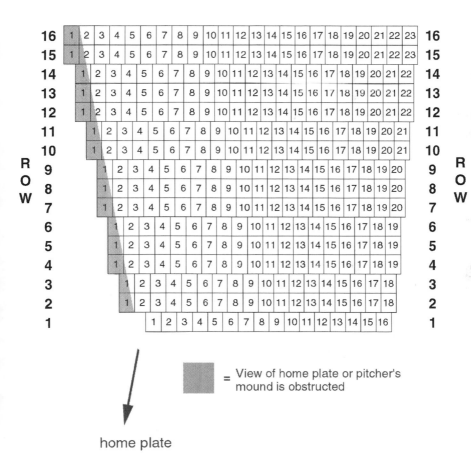

= View of home plate or pitcher's mound is obstructed

home plate

Section 23

Infield Grandstand
Face Value of tickets is $52

Section 23 is near home plate and
behind Loge Boxes 135-136 and Field
Boxes 50-51.

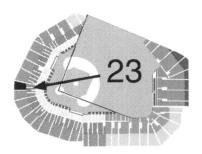

Section 23 is an excellent section. It is
near home plate and offers a great
view of the entire park.

There is a pole which obstructs the view the higher numbered seats on the
end of the rows. Any seat numbered 15 or lower is safe from poles.

The view from the center of Section 23

Section 23

ROW		Wheelchair Seating Row (Installed prior to 2009 season)																						ROW
17																									17
14	1	2	3	4	5	6	7	8	9	10	11	12	13	14	15	16	17	18	19	20	21	22			14
13	1	2	3	4	5	6	7	8	9	10	11	12	13	14	15	16	17	18	19	20	21	22			13
12	1	2	3	4	5	6	7	8	9	10	11	12	13	14	15	16	17	18	19	20	21				12
11	1	2	3	4	5	6	7	8	9	10	11	12	13	14	15	16	17	18	19	20	21				11
10	1	2	3	4	5	6	7	8	9	10	11	12	13	14	15	16	17	18	19	20	21				10
9	1	2	3	4	5	6	7	8	9	10	11	12	13	14	15	16	17	18	19	20					9
8	1	2	3	4	5	6	7	8	9	10	11	12	13	14	15	16	17	18	19	20					8
7	1	2	3	4	5	6	7	8	9	10	11	12	13	14	15	16	17	18	19	20					7
6	1	2	3	4	5	6	7	8	9	10	11	12	13	14	15	16	17	18	19						6
5	1	2	3	4	5	6	7	8	9	10	11	12	13	14	15	16	17	18	19						5
4	1	2	3	4	5	6	7	8	9	10	11	12	13	14	15	16	17	18							4
3	1	2	3	4	5	6	7	8	9	10	11	12	13	14	15	16	17	18							3
2	1	2	3	4	5	6	7	8	9	10	11	12	13	14	15	16	17	18							2
1	1	2	3	4	5	6	7	8	9	10	11	12	13	14	15	16									1

= View of home plate or pitcher's mound is obstructed

home plate

Section 24

Infield Grandstand
Face Value of tickets is $52

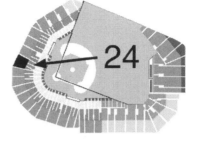

Section 24 is near the visiting team's
on deck circle and behind Loge Boxes
137-140 and Field Boxes 51-55.

Section 24 is one of the best
Grandstand sections in the park for
viewing a game. Seats in the center of the section look directly down the
first base line and are very close to the action.

Only a handful of seats in the upper rows at the very end of each row are
affected by pole issues.

The view from the center of Section 24

Section 24

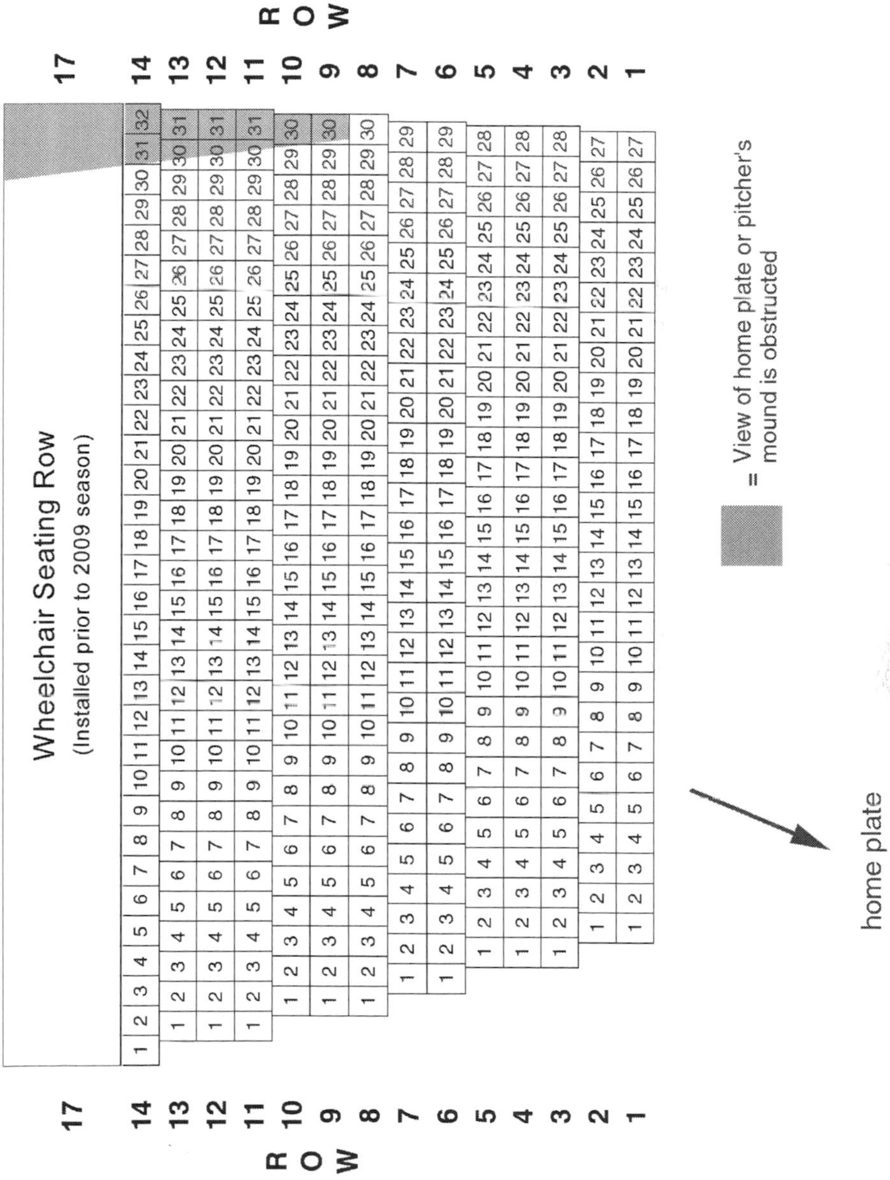

R O W

17 14 13 12 11 10 9 8 7 6 5 4 3 2 1

Wheelchair Seating Row
(Installed prior to 2009 season)

= View of home plate or pitcher's mound is obstructed

home plate

17 14 13 12 11 10 9 8 7 6 5 4 3 2 1

R O W

Section 25

Infield Grandstand
Face Value of tickets is $52

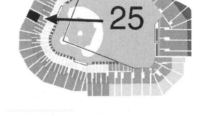

Section 25 is in between home plate
and third base and behind Loge Boxes
141-144 and Field Boxes 56-60.

Section 25 is an excellent section for
viewing the game. With the vast
majority of the seats free from obstructions, you really have a nice view of
the infield and the entire park from this section.

Only the first two seats in each row have pole issues.

The view from the center of Section 25

Section 25

ROW																									ROW
16	1	2	3	4	5	6	7	8	9	10	11	12	13	14	15	16	17	18	19	20	21	22	23		**16**
15	1	2	3	4	5	6	7	8	9	10	11	12	13	14	15	16	17	18	19	20	21	22	23	24	**15**
14	1	2	3	4	5	6	7	8	9	10	11	12	13	14	15	16	17	18	19	20	21	22	23	24	**14**
13	1	2	3	4	5	6	7	8	9	10	11	12	13	14	15	16	17	18	19	20	21	22	23	24	**13**
12	1	2	3	4	5	6	7	8	9	10	11	12	13	14	15	16	17	18	19	20	21	22	23	24	**12**
11	1	2	3	4	5	6	7	8	9	10	11	12	13	14	15	16	17	18	19	20	21	22	23	24	**11**
10	1	2	3	4	5	6	7	8	9	10	11	12	13	14	15	16	17	18	19	20	21	22	23	24	**10**
9	1	2	3	4	5	6	7	8	9	10	11	12	13	14	15	16	17	18	19	20	21	22	23	24	**9**
8	1	2	3	4	5	6	7	8	9	10	11	12	13	14	15	16	17	18	19	20	21	22	23	24	**8**
7	1	2	3	4	5	6	7	8	9	10	11	12	13	14	15	16	17	18	19	20	21	22	23	24	**7**
6	1	2	3	4	5	6	7	8	9	10	11	12	13	14	15	16	17	18	19	20	21	22	23	24	**6**
5	1	2	3	4	5	6	7	8	9	10	11	12	13	14	15	16	17	18	19	20	21	22	23	24	**5**
4	1	2	3	4	5	6	7	8	9	10	11	12	13	14	15	16	17	18	19	20	21	22	23	24	**4**
3	1	2	3	4	5	6	7	8	9	10	11	12	13	14	15	16	17	18	19	20	21	22	23	24	**3**
2	1	2	3	4	5	6	7	8	9	10	11	12	13	14	15	16	17	18	19	20	21	22	23	24	**2**
1	1	2	3	4	5	6	7	8	9	10	11	12	13	14	15	16	17	18	19	20	21	22	23		**1**

home plate

 = View of home plate or pitcher's mound is obstructed

Section 26

Infield Grandstand
Face Value of tickets is $52

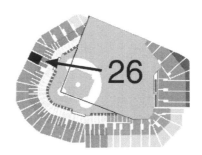

Section 26 is near third base and the visiting team's dugout. It is behind Loge Boxes 145-148 and Field Boxes 61-64.

Section 26 is a very good section for viewing the game. It is very close to the infield but also has a nice view of the Monster.

Pole issues in this section run diagonally from bottom right to seats in the middle of the top rows if you are facing the field. The pole issues in the first few rows with the lowest seat numbers are particularly problematic. The first two seats in rows 10 through 18 are also obstructed.

The view from the center of Section 26

Section 26

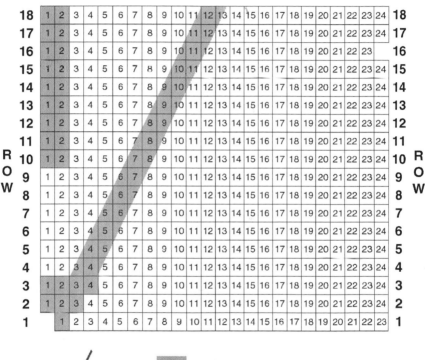

home plate

= View of home plate or pitcher's mound is obstructed

Section 27

Infield Grandstand
Face Value of tickets is $52

Section 27 is just past third base on the left field line. It is behind Loge Boxes 149-151 and Field Boxes 65-68.

Section 27 is a very good section for viewing the game. It is close to the infield but also has a good view of the Monster.

Pole issues in this section run diagonally from bottom right to top left if you are facing the field. The pole issues in the first few rows with the lowest seat numbers are particularly problematic.

The view from the center of Section 27

Section 27

18	1	2	3	4	5	6	7	8	9	10	11	12	13	14	15	16	17	18	19	20	21	22	23	24		18
17	1	2	3	4	5	6	7	8	9	10	11	12	13	14	15	16	17	18	19	20	21	22	23	24		17
16	1	2	3	4	5	6	7	8	9	10	11	12	13	14	15	16	17	18	19	20	21	22	23	24		16
15	1	2	3	4	5	6	7	8	9	10	11	12	13	14	15	16	17	18	19	20	21	22	23	24		15
14	1	2	3	4	5	6	7	8	9	10	11	12	13	14	15	16	17	18	19	20	21	22	23	24		14
13	1	2	3	4	5	6	7	8	9	10	11	12	13	14	15	16	17	18	19	20	21	22	23	24	25	13
12	1	2	3	4	5	6	7	8	9	10	11	12	13	14	15	16	17	18	19	20	21	22	23	24	25	12
11	1	2	3	4	5	6	7	8	9	10	11	12	13	14	15	16	17	18	19	20	21	22	23	24	25	11
10	1	2	3	4	5	6	7	8	9	10	11	12	13	14	15	16	17	18	19	20	21	22	23	24	25	10
9	1	2	3	4	5	6	7	8	9	10	11	12	13	14	15	16	17	18	19	20	21	22	23	24	25	9
8	1	2	3	4	5	6	7	8	9	10	11	12	13	14	15	16	17	18	19	20	21	22	23	24	25	8
7	1	2	3	4	5	6	7	8	9	10	11	12	13	14	15	16	17	18	19	20	21	22	23	24	25	7
6	1	2	3	4	5	6	7	8	9	10	11	12	13	14	15	16	17	18	19	20	21	22	23	24	25	6
5	1	2	3	4	5	6	7	8	9	10	11	12	13	14	15	16	17	18	19	20	21	22	23	24	25	5
4	1	2	3	4	5	6	7	8	9	10	11	12	13	14	15	16	17	18	19	20	21	22	23	24	25	4
3	1	2	3	4	5	6	7	8	9	10	11	12	13	14	15	16	17	18	19	20	21	22	23	24	25	3
2	1	2	3	4	5	6	7	8	9	10	11	12	13	14	15	16	17	18	19	20	21	22	23	24	25	2
1		1	2	3	4	5	6	7	8	9	10	11	12	13	14	15	16	17	18	19	20	21	22	23		1

(Left and right margins labeled **R O W**)

 = View of home plate or pitcher's mound is obstructed

home plate

Section 28

Infield Grandstand
Face Value of tickets is $52

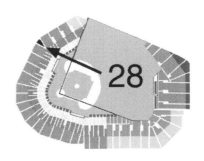

Section 28 is in just past third base on the left field line and is behind Loge Box 152 and Field Box 69.

Perhaps the most oddly shaped section in the park, 28 is basically a triangle. The first row is Row 3 and it has only one seat. The unusual shape is due to the fact that 28 is the junction between the sections that are parallel to the third base line (24-27) and the sections that turn so they can face the infield (29-33).

Pole issues are limited to upper row seats on the left and right sides of the section.

The view from the center of Section 28

Section 28

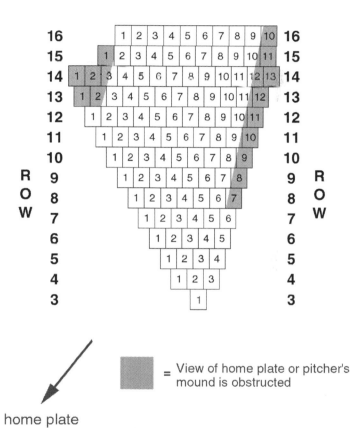

= View of home plate or pitcher's mound is obstructed

home plate

Section 29

Infield Grandstand
Face Value of tickets is $52

Section 29 is past third base on the left field line and is behind Loge Boxes 153-156 and Field Boxes 70-71.

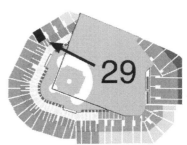

It is an excellent section for viewing the game. The seats are close to the Green Monster and you are still fairly close to the infield.

A pole affects seats 1 and 2 in the first row and the obstruction runs diagonally up to seats 5 and 6 in row 18. The last seat in rows 3 and 4 are also affected.

The view from the center of Section 29

128

Section 29

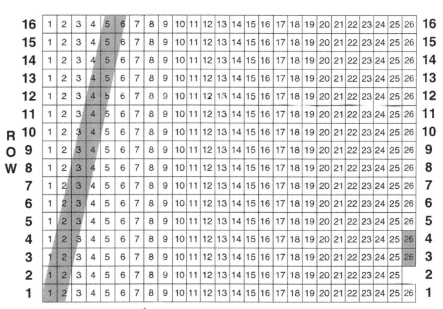

home plate

= View of home plate or pitcher's mound is obstructed

Section 30

Infield Grandstand
Face Value of tickets is $52

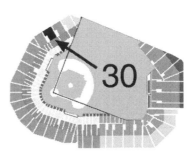

Section 30 is on the left field line between third base and the Green Monster and is behind Loge Boxes 157-159 and Field Boxes 72-76.

It is a very good section for viewing the game. The seats are close to the Green Monster and not too far from the infield.

Only a few seats have pole issues. If you are facing the field these are on the right side of the section in rows 8 through 15. Seat 19 in row 2 is also affected.

The view from the center of Section 30

Section 30

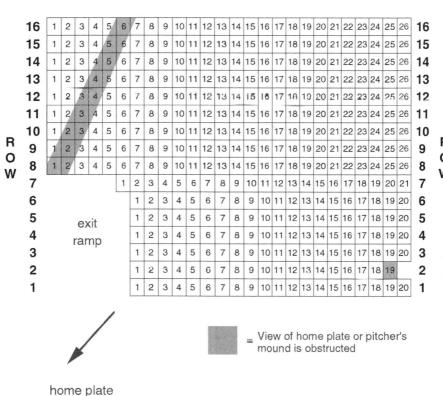

= View of home plate or pitcher's mound is obstructed

home plate

Section 31

Infield Grandstand
Face Value of tickets is $52

Section 31 is on the left field line near
the Green Monster and is behind Loge
Boxes 160-161 and Field Boxes 77-82.

While it is a good section for viewing
the game, be aware that it is further
from home plate than any other section on the left side that is classified as
Infield Grandstand. If you are one section over in Section 32, the face value
of tickets drops to $30.

If you are facing the field, pole issues are limited to seats on the right in
rows 8 through 16. All seats in the first 7 rows are not affected by poles,
and in rows 8 through 16, any seats numbered higher than 11 are safe from
poles.

The view from the center of Section 31

132

Section 31

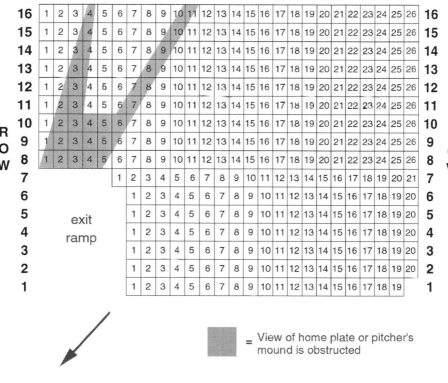

exit ramp

home plate

= View of home plate or pitcher's mound is obstructed

Section 32

Outfield Grandstand
Face Value of tickets is $30
No alcohol section

Section 32 is on the left field line near
the Green Monster and is behind Loge
Box 162-163.

Along with section 33, this is one of
best value sections in the park. With seats priced at only $30, it is in an
excellent position to view the game and the entire park. There are Loge Box
seats in front of Section 32, but no Field Box seats, which makes these seats
some of the closest to the field of any grandstand section.

Rows 1 through 7 are not affected by poles, but some seats on the right side
of the section if you are facing the field are affected. Please be aware that
seats 3 through 6 in row 1 are often affected by wheelchair seating in front
of them.

The view from the center of Section 32

Section 32

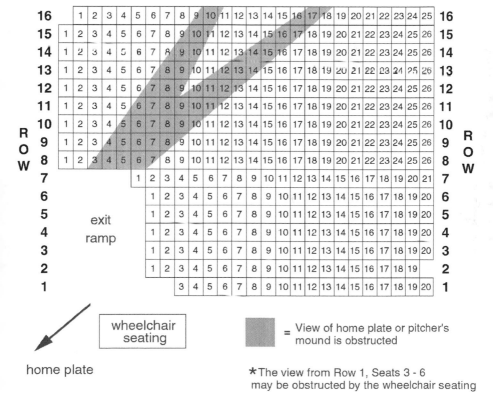

ROW																											ROW
16	1	2	3	4	5	6	7	8	9	10	11	12	13	14	15	16	17	18	19	20	21	22	23	24	25		16
15	1	2	3	4	5	6	7	8	9	10	11	12	13	14	15	16	17	18	19	20	21	22	23	24	25	26	15
14	1	2	3	4	5	6	7	8	9	10	11	12	13	14	15	16	17	18	19	20	21	22	23	24	25	26	14
13	1	2	3	4	5	6	7	8	9	10	11	12	13	14	15	16	17	18	19	20	21	22	23	24	25	26	13
12	1	2	3	4	5	6	7	8	9	10	11	12	13	14	15	16	17	18	19	20	21	22	23	24	25	26	12
11	1	2	3	4	5	6	7	8	9	10	11	12	13	14	15	16	17	18	19	20	21	22	23	24	25	26	11
10	1	2	3	4	5	6	7	8	9	10	11	12	13	14	15	16	17	18	19	20	21	22	23	24	25	26	10
9	1	2	3	4	5	6	7	8	9	10	11	12	13	14	15	16	17	18	19	20	21	22	23	24	25	26	9
8	1	2	3	4	5	6	7	8	9	10	11	12	13	14	15	16	17	18	19	20	21	22	23	24	25	26	8
7			1	2	3	4	5	6	7	8	9	10	11	12	13	14	15	16	17	18	19	20	21				7
6			1	2	3	4	5	6	7	8	9	10	11	12	13	14	15	16	17	18	19	20					6
5			1	2	3	4	5	6	7	8	9	10	11	12	13	14	15	16	17	18	19	20					5
4			1	2	3	4	5	6	7	8	9	10	11	12	13	14	15	16	17	18	19	20					4
3			1	2	3	4	5	6	7	8	9	10	11	12	13	14	15	16	17	18	19	20					3
2			1	2	3	4	5	6	7	8	9	10	11	12	13	14	15	16	17	18	19						2
1				3	4	5	6	7	8	9	10	11	12	13	14	15	16	17	18	19	20						1

exit ramp

wheelchair seating

= View of home plate or pitcher's mound is obstructed

home plate

*The view from Row 1, Seats 3 - 6 may be obstructed by the wheelchair seating

Section 33

Outfield Grandstand
Face Value of tickets is $30
No alcohol section

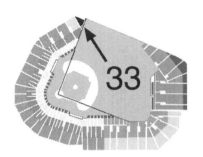

Section 33 is down the left field line
next to the Green Monster and behind
Loge Box 163.

33 is a triangular treasure tucked into
the left field corner next to the Monster. It is the closest Grandstand
section to the field, with only 1 to 3 rows of Loge Box seats in front of it.
And, if you sit in row 3, seat 16, you can actually touch the Monster and the
left field foul pole from your seat. This is the same pole off which Pudge
Fisk hit his classic 1975 World Series home run.

Pole issues in this section run across the middle rows. If you have any seats
in the first three rows you have no pole issues.

The view from the center of Section 33

Section 33

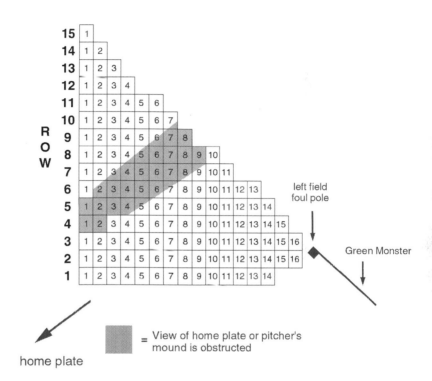

left field
foul pole

Green Monster

■ = View of home plate or pitcher's
    mound is obstructed

home plate

How Far from the Field are My Seats?

If you are sitting on the main seating level, there is a very good chance that you will have no idea how far from the field your seats will be. Where exactly is Loge Box 102, row GG? The location information on the ticket gives you very little idea as to where you will be sitting. With the information in this chapter you will be able to tell not only where that row is located, but exactly how many rows it is from the field. **Use this chapter when buying tickets so you will know where you will be sitting.**

The column to the right of each row letter is entitled "From Field." The number in this column tells you how many rows from the field you seats will be. To take an example from page 139, Row AA of Right Field Box 86 is 11 rows from the field.

Section Finder

There are only two rows in the following sections: Dugout Box, Extended Dugout Box, and the Canvas Alley Dugout Box. If you have seats in one of these areas you will know you are only one or two rows from the field.

Right Field Box

The Right Field Box sections curl around the right field corner, starting next to the visitor's bullpen and bleachers on one end and stopping at Canvas Alley*, which is midway between the infield and the right field foul pole, known as Pesky's Pole.

*Canvas Alley is a ground-level alley where the field maintenance crew sits during games. It is the traditional demarcation line between the infield and outfield seats on the first base side of the field.

Right Field Box 86
RFB Box 86 is on the field facing home plate and it has 13 rows

Row	From Field	Row	From Field	Row	From Field
A1	on the field	E	6 rows	AA	11 rows
A	2 rows	F	7 rows	BB	12 rows
B	3 rows	G	8 rows	CC	13 rows
C	4 rows	H	9 rows		
D	5 rows	J	10 rows		

Right Field Box 87
RFB 87 starts on the field and extends back to the beginning of Grandstand Section 1. It has 31 Rows and is split into two sections, with 13 rows in the front section and 18 rows in the back

Row	From Field	Row	From Field	Row	From Field
A1	on the field	AA	11 rows	MM	21 rows
A	2 rows	BB	12 rows	NN	22 rows
B	3 rows	CC	13 rows	PP	23 rows
C	4 rows	start of back section		QQ	24 rows
D	5 rows	EE	14 rows	RR	25 rows
E	6 rows	FF	15 rows	SS	26 rows
F	7 rows	GG	16 rows	TT	27 rows
G	8 rows	HH	17 rows	UU	28 rows
H	9 rows	JJ	18 rows	VV	29 rows
J	10 rows	KK	19 rows	WW	30 rows
		LL	20 rows	XX	31 rows

Right Field Box 88
RFB 88 is located behind boxes 86 and 87 and faces home plate. It has 18 rows and extends back to the beginning of Grandstand Section 2.

Row	From Field	Row	From Field	Row	From Field
EE	14 rows	LL	20 rows	SS	26 rows
FF	15 rows	MM	21 rows	TT	27 rows
GG	16 rows	NN	22 rows	UU	28 rows
HH	17 rows	PP	23 rows	VV	29 rows
JJ	18 rows	QQ	24 rows	WW	30 rows
KK	19 rows	RR	25 rows	XX	31 rows

Right Field Box 89
RFB 89 is located behind box 86 and faces the third base line. It has 18 rows and extends back to the beginning of Grandstand Section 3.

Row	From Field	Row	From Field	Row	From Field
EE	14 rows	GG	16 rows	JJ	18 rows
FF	15 rows	HH	17 rows	KK	19 rows

LL	20 rows	QQ	24 rows	UU	28 rows		
MM	21 rows	RR	25 rows	VV	29 rows		
NN	22 rows	SS	26 rows	WW	30 rows		
PP	23 rows	TT	27 rows	XX	31 rows		

Right Field Box 90

RFB 90 is located behind box 86 and faces left field. It has 18 rows and extends back to the beginning of Grandstand Section 4.

Row	From Field	Row	From Field	Row	From Field
EE	13 rows	LL	19 rows	SS	25 rows
FF	14 rows	MM	20 rows	TT	26 rows
GG	15 rows	NN	21 rows	UU	27 rows
HH	16 rows	PP	22 rows	VV	28 rows
JJ	17 rows	QQ	23 rows	WW	29 rows
KK	18 rows	RR	24 rows	XX	30 rows

Right Field Box 91

RFB 91 is located behind box 86 and faces leftcenter field. It has 18 rows and extends back to the beginning of Grandstand Section 5.

Row	From Field	Row	From Field	Row	From Field
EE	13 rows	LL	19 rows	SS	25 rows
FF	14 rows	MM	20 rows	TT	26 rows
GG	15 rows	NN	21 rows	UU	27 rows
HH	16 rows	PP	22 rows	VV	28 rows
JJ	17 rows	QQ	23 rows	WW	29 rows
KK	18 rows	RR	24 rows	XX	30 rows

Right Field Box 92

RFB 92 is located on the field and faces leftcenter field. It has 30 rows and extends back to the beginning of Grandstand Section 6. Row B has only 1 seat.

Row	From Field	Row	From Field	Row	From Field
B	on the field	CC	11 rows	NN	21 rows
C	2 rows	DD	12 rows	PP	22 rows
D	3 rows	EE	13 rows	QQ	23 rows
E	4 rows	FF	14 rows	RR	24 rows
F	5 rows	GG	15 rows	SS	25 rows
G	6 rows	HH	16 rows	TT	26 rows
H	7 rows	JJ	17 rows	UU	27 rows
J	8 rows	KK	18 rows	VV	28 rows
AA	9 rows	LL	19 rows	WW	29 rows
BB	10 rows	MM	20 rows	XX	30 rows

Right Field Box 93

RFB 93 is located on the field and faces leftcenter field. It has 27 rows and extends back to the beginning of Grandstand Section 7.

Row	From Field	Row	From Field	Row	From Field
E	on the field	EE	10 rows	PP	19 rows
F	2 rows	FF	11 rows	QQ	20 rows
G	3 rows	GG	12 rows	RR	21 rows
H	4 rows	HH	13 rows	SS	22 rows
J	5 rows	JJ	14 rows	TT	23 rows
AA	6 rows	KK	15 rows	UU	24 rows
BB	7 rows	LL	16 rows	VV	25 rows
CC	8 rows	MM	17 rows	WW	26 rows
DD	9 rows	NN	18 rows	XX	27 rows

Right Field Box 94

RFB 94 is located partially on the field and partially behind Right Field Boxes 1AA and 1AAA. It faces leftcenter field, has 27 rows and extends back to the beginning of Grandstand Section 8. Seats 3, 4,and 5 in row E are right next to the Pesky Pole.

Row	From Field	Row	From Field	Row	From Field
E	on the field	EE	10 rows	PP	19 rows
F	2 rows	FF	11 rows	QQ	20 rows
G	3 rows	GG	12 rows	RR	21 rows
H	4 rows	HH	13 rows	SS	22 rows
J	5 rows	JJ	14 rows	TT	23 rows
AA	6 rows	KK	15 rows	UU	24 rows
BB	7 rows	LL	16 rows	VV	25 rows
CC	8 rows	MM	17 rows	WW	26 rows
DD	9 rows	NN	18 rows	XX	27 rows

Right Field Box 95/96

RFB 95/96 is located behind Canvas Alley Dugout Boxes (2 rows) and Right Field Boxes 1 and 3 (9 Rows). So the first row in RFB 95/96 is 12 rows from the field. RFB 95/96 has 22 rows, faces leftcenter field and extends back to the beginning of Grandstand Section 9.

Row	From Field	Row	From Field	Row	From Field
AA	12 rows	JJ	20 rows	SS	28 rows
BB	13 rows	KK	21 rows	TT	29 rows
CC	14 rows	LL	22 rows	UU	30 rows
DD	15 rows	MM	23 rows	VV	31 rows
EE	16 rows	NN	24 rows	WW	32 rows
FF	17 rows	PP	25 rows	XX	33 rows
GG	18 rows	QQ	26 rows		
HH	19 rows	RR	27 rows		

Right Field Box 97

RFB 97 is located behind Canvas Alley Dugout Boxes (2 rows) and Right Field Boxes 5 and 7 (9 Rows). So the first row in RFB 97 is 12 rows from the field. RFB 97 has 22 rows, faces leftcenter field and extends back to the beginning of Grandstand Section 10.

Row	From Field	Row	From Field	Row	From Field
AA	12 rows	JJ	20 rows	SS	28 rows
BB	13 rows	KK	21 rows	TT	29 rows
CC	14 rows	LL	22 rows	UU	30 rows
DD	15 rows	MM	23 rows	VV	31 rows
EE	16 rows	NN	24 rows	WW	32 rows
FF	17 rows	PP	25 rows	XX	33 rows
GG	18 rows	QQ	26 rows		
HH	19 rows	RR	27 rows		

Loge Box

The Loge Box sections are located between the Field Box and Grandstand sections. They start a little way past first base at Box 98 on the right field line and go all the way around the infield, ending near the Green Monster in Box 165.

In most of the Loge Box sections the first few rows can be affected by the walkways in front of the sections. Fans going to and from their seats during the game can cause an annoying distraction and obstruction if you sit in these seats. The rows that are affected by the walkways are marked **Walk** in the tables below.

Loge Box 98

Rows: 13
Behind: Extended Dugout Boxes and Field Box 9
In front of: Grandstand Section 11

Row	From Field	Row	From Field	Row	From Field
DD	18 rows	JJ	23 rows	PP	28 rows
EE	19 rows	KK	24 rows	QQ	29 rows
FF	20 rows	LL	25 rows	RR	30 rows
GG	21 rows	MM	26 rows		
HH	22 rows	NN	27 rows		

Loge Box 99

Rows: 16
Behind: Extended Dugout Boxes and Field Box 10
In front of: Grandstand Section 11
Note: Walkway advisory in first 3 rows

Row	From Field	Row	From Field	Row	From Field
AA	15 Walk	GG	21 rows	NN	27 rows
BB	16 Walk	HH	22 rows	PP	28 rows
CC	17 Walk	JJ	23 rows	QQ	29 rows
DD	18 rows	KK	24 rows	RR	30 rows
EE	19 rows	LL	25 rows		
FF	20 rows	MM	26 rows		

Loge Box 100

Rows: 16
Behind: Extended Dugout Boxes and Field Box 11
In front of: Grandstand Section 11
Note: Walkway advisory in first 3 rows

Row	From Field	Row	From Field	Row	From Field
AA	15 Walk	GG	21 rows	NN	27 rows
BB	16 Walk	HH	22 rows	PP	28 rows
CC	17 Walk	JJ	23 rows	QQ	29 rows
DD	18 rows	KK	24 rows	RR	30 rows
EE	19 rows	LL	25 rows		
FF	20 rows	MM	26 rows		

Loge Box 101

Rows: 16
Behind: Extended Dugout Boxes and Field Box 13
In front of: Grandstand Section 12
Note: Walkway advisory in first 3 rows

Row	From Field	Row	From Field	Row	From Field
AA	15 Walk	GG	21 rows	NN	27 rows
BB	16 Walk	HH	22 rows	PP	28 rows
CC	17 Walk	JJ	23 rows	QQ	29 rows
DD	18 rows	KK	24 rows	RR	30 rows
EE	19 rows	LL	25 rows		
FF	20 rows	MM	26 rows		

Loge Box 102

Rows: 16
Behind: Extended Dugout Boxes and Field Box 14
In front of: Grandstand Section 12
Note: Walkway advisory in first 3 rows

Row	From Field	Row	From Field	Row	From Field
AA	15 Walk	GG	21 rows	NN	27 rows
BB	16 Walk	HH	22 rows	PP	28 rows
CC	17 Walk	JJ	23 rows	QQ	29 rows
DD	18 rows	KK	24 rows	RR	30 rows
EE	19 rows	LL	25 rows		
FF	20 rows	MM	26 rows		

Loge Box 103

Rows: 16
Behind: Extended Dugout Boxes and Field Boxes 15 and 16
In front of: Grandstand Section 12
Note: Walkway advisory in first 3 rows

Row	From Field	Row	From Field	Row	From Field
AA	15 Walk	GG	21 rows	NN	27 rows
BB	16 Walk	HH	22 rows	PP	28 rows
CC	17 Walk	JJ	23 rows	QQ	29 rows
DD	18 rows	KK	24 rows	RR	30 rows
EE	19 rows	LL	25 rows		
FF	20 rows	MM	26 rows		

Loge Box 104

Rows: 10
Behind: Field Box 17
In front of: Grandstand Section 12

Row	From Field	Row	From Field	Row	From Field
GG	19 rows	LL	23 rows	QQ	27 rows
HH	20 rows	MM	24 rows	RR	28 rows
JJ	21 rows	NN	25 rows		
KK	22 rows	PP	26 rows		

Loge Box 105

Rows: 16
Behind: Field Boxes 18 and 19
In front of: Grandstand Section 13
Note: Walkway advisory in first 3 rows

Row	From Field	Row	From Field	Row	From Field
AA	13 Walk	BB	14 Walk	CC	15 Walk

DD	16 rows	JJ	21 rows	PP	26 rows
EE	17 rows	KK	22 rows	QQ	27 rows
FF	18 rows	LL	23 rows	RR	28 rows
GG	19 rows	MM	24 rows		
HH	20 rows	NN	25 rows		

Loge Box 106

Rows: 16
Behind: Field Box 20
In front of: Grandstand Section 13
Note: Walkway advisory in first 3 rows

Row	From Field	Row	From Field	Row	From Field
AA	13 Walk	GG	19 rows	NN	25 rows
BB	14 Walk	HH	20 rows	PP	26 rows
CC	15 Walk	JJ	21 rows	QQ	27 rows
DD	16 rows	KK	22 rows	RR	28 rows
EE	17 rows	LL	23 rows		
FF	18 rows	MM	24 rows		

Loge Box 107

Rows: 13
Behind: Red Sox dugout and Field Box 21
In front of: Grandstand Section 14
Note: Walkway advisory in first 3 rows

Row	From Field	Row	From Field	Row	From Field
AA	11 Walk	FF	16 rows	LL	21 rows
BB	12 Walk	GG	17 rows	MM	22 rows
CC	13 Walk	HH	18 rows	NN	23 rows
DD	14 rows	JJ	19 rows		
EE	15 rows	KK	20 rows		

Loge Box 108

Rows: 13
Behind: Red Sox dugout and Field Box 21
In front of: Grandstand Section 14
Note: Walkway advisory in first 3 rows

Row	From Field	Row	From Field	Row	From Field
AA	11 Walk	FF	16 rows	LL	21 rows
BB	12 Walk	GG	17 rows	MM	22 rows
CC	13 Walk	HH	18 rows	NN	23 rows
DD	14 rows	JJ	19 rows		
EE	15 rows	KK	20 rows		

Loge Box 109

Rows: 13
Behind: Red Sox dugout and Field Box 22
In front of: Grandstand Section 14
Note: Walkway advisory in first 3 rows

Row	From Field	Row	From Field	Row	From Field
AA	11 Walk	FF	16 rows	LL	21 rows
BB	12 Walk	GG	17 rows	MM	22 rows
CC	13 Walk	HH	18 rows	NN	23 rows
DD	14 rows	JJ	19 rows		
EE	15 rows	KK	20 rows		

Loge Box 110

Rows: 13
Behind: Red Sox dugout and Field Box 23
In front of: Grandstand Section 14
Note: Walkway advisory in first 3 rows

Row	From Field	Row	From Field	Row	From Field
AA	11 Walk	FF	16 rows	LL	21 rows
BB	12 Walk	GG	17 rows	MM	22 rows
CC	13 Walk	HH	18 rows	NN	23 rows
DD	14 rows	JJ	19 rows		
EE	15 rows	KK	20 rows		

Loge Box 111

Rows: 13
Behind: Red Sox dugout and Field Box 24
In front of: Grandstand Section 14
Note: Walkway advisory in first 3 rows

Row	From Field	Row	From Field	Row	From Field
AA	11 Walk	FF	16 rows	LL	21 rows
BB	12 Walk	GG	17 rows	MM	22 rows
CC	13 Walk	HH	18 rows	NN	23 rows
DD	14 rows	JJ	19 rows		
EE	15 rows	KK	20 rows		

Loge Box 112

Rows: 13
Behind: Red Sox dugout and Field Box 25
In front of: Grandstand Section 15
Note: Walkway advisory in first 3 rows

Row	From Field	Row	From Field	Row	From Field
AA	11 Walk	BB	12 Walk	CC	13 Walk

DD	14 rows	HH	18 rows	MM	22 rows
EE	15 rows	JJ	19 rows	NN	23 rows
FF	16 rows	KK	20 rows		
GG	17 rows	LL	21 rows		

Loge Box 113
Rows: 13
Behind: Red Sox dugout and Field Boxes 26 and 27
In front of: Grandstand Section 15
Note: Walkway advisory in first 3 rows

Row	From Field	Row	From Field	Row	From Field
AA	11 Walk	FF	16 rows	LL	21 rows
BB	12 Walk	GG	17 rows	MM	22 rows
CC	13 Walk	HH	18 rows	NN	23 rows
DD	14 rows	JJ	19 rows		
EE	15 rows	KK	20 rows		

Loge Box 114
Rows: 13
Behind: Red Sox dugout and Field Box 28
In front of: Grandstand Section 15
Note: Walkway advisory in first 3 rows

Row	From Field	Row	From Field	Row	From Field
AA	11 Walk	FF	16 rows	LL	21 rows
BB	12 Walk	GG	17 rows	MM	22 rows
CC	13 Walk	HH	18 rows	NN	23 rows
DD	14 rows	JJ	19 rows		
EE	15 rows	KK	20 rows		

Loge Box 115
Rows: 13
Behind: Infield Dugout Boxes and Field Box 29
In front of: Grandstand Section 15
Note: Walkway advisory in first 3 rows

Row	From Field	Row	From Field	Row	From Field
AA	15 Walk	FF	20 rows	LL	25 rows
BB	16 Walk	GG	21 rows	MM	26 rows
CC	17 Walk	HH	22 rows	NN	27 rows
DD	18 rows	JJ	23 rows		
EE	19 rows	KK	24 rows		

Loge Box 116
Rows: 8
Behind: Infield Dugout Boxes and Field Box 30
In front of: Grandstand Section 16

Row	From Field	Row	From Field	Row	From Field
FF	20 rows	JJ	23 rows	MM	26
GG	21 rows	KK	24 rows	NN	27
HH	22 rows	LL	25 rows		

Loge Box 117
Rows: 13
Behind: Infield Dugout Boxes and Field Box 31
In front of: Grandstand Section 16
Note: Walkway advisory in first 3 rows

Row	From Field	Row	From Field	Row	From Field
AA	15 Walk	FF	20 rows	LL	25 rows
BB	16 Walk	GG	21 rows	MM	26 rows
CC	17 Walk	HH	22 rows	NN	27 rows
DD	18 rows	JJ	23 rows		
EE	19 rows	KK	24 rows		

Loge Box 118
Rows: 13
Behind: Infield Dugout Boxes and Field Box 32
In front of: Grandstand Section 16
Note: Walkway advisory in first 3 rows

Row	From Field	Row	From Field	Row	From Field
AA	15 Walk	FF	20 rows	LL	25 rows
BB	16 Walk	GG	21 rows	MM	26 rows
CC	17 Walk	HH	22 rows	NN	27 rows
DD	18 rows	JJ	23 rows		
EE	19 rows	KK	24v		

Loge Box 119
Rows: 13
Behind: Infield Dugout Boxes and Field Box 33
In front of: Grandstand Section 16
Note: Walkway advisory in first 3 rows

Row	From Field	Row	From Field	Row	From Field
AA	15 Walk	DD	18 rows	GG	21 rows
BB	16 Walk	EE	19 rows	HH	22 rows
CC	17 Walk	FF	20 rows	JJ	23 rows

KK	24 rows	MM	26 rows
LL	25 rows	NN	27 rows

Loge Box 120

Rows: 13
Behind: Infield Dugout Boxes and Field Box 34
In front of: Grandstand Section 16
Note: Walkway advisory in first 3 rows

Row	From Field	Row	From Field	Row	From Field
AA	15 Walk	FF	20 rows	LL	25 rows
BB	16 Walk	GG	21 rows	MM	26 rows
CC	17 Walk	HH	22 rows	NN	27 rows
DD	18 rows	JJ	23 rows		
EE	19 rows	KK	24 rows		

Loge Box 121

Rows: 13
Behind: Infield Dugout Boxes and Field Boxes 35 and 36
In front of: Grandstand Section 17
Note: Walkway advisory in first 3 rows

Row	From Field	Row	From Field	Row	From Field
AA	15 Walk	FF	20 rows	LL	25 rows
BB	16 Walk	GG	21 rows	MM	26 rows
CC	17 Walk	HH	22 rows	NN	27 rows
DD	18 rows	JJ	23 rows		
EE	19 rows	KK	24 rows		

Loge Box 122

Rows: 13
Behind: Infield Dugout Boxes and Field Box 37
In front of: Grandstand Section 17
Note: Walkway advisory in first 3 rows

Row	From Field	Row	From Field	Row	From Field
AA	15 Walk	FF	20 rows	LL	25 rows
BB	16 Walk	GG	21 rows	MM	26 rows
CC	17 Walk	HH	22 rows	NN	27 rows
DD	18 rows	JJ	23 rows		
EE	19 rows	KK	24 rows		

Loge Box 123

Rows: 13
Behind: Infield Dugout Boxes and Field Box 38
In front of: Grandstand Section 17
Note: Walkway advisory in first 3 rows

Row	From Field	Row	From Field	Row	From Field
AA	15 Walk	FF	20 rows	LL	25 rows
BB	16 Walk	GG	21 rows	MM	26 rows
CC	17 Walk	HH	22 rows	NN	27 rows
DD	18 rows	JJ	23 rows		
EE	19 rows	KK	24 rows		

Loge Box 124

Rows: 13
Behind: Infield Dugout Boxes and Field Box 38
In front of: Grandstand Section 17
Note: Walkway advisory in first 3 rows

Row	From Field	Row	From Field	Row	From Field
AA	15 Walk	FF	20 rows	LL	25 rows
BB	16 Walk	GG	21 rows	MM	26 rows
CC	17 Walk	HH	22 rows	NN	27 rows
DD	18 rows	JJ	23 rows		
EE	19 rows	KK	24 rows		

Loge Box 125

Rows: 13
Behind: Infield Dugout Boxes and Field Box 39
In front of: Grandstand Section 18
Note: Walkway advisory in first 3 rows

Row	From Field	Row	From Field	Row	From Field
AA	15 Walk	FF	20 rows	LL	25 rows
BB	16 Walk	GG	21 rows	MM	26 rows
CC	17 Walk	HH	22 rows	NN	27 rows
DD	18 rows	JJ	23 rows		
EE	19 rows	KK	24 rows		

Loge Box 126

Rows: 13
Behind: Infield Dugout Boxes and Field Box 40
In front of: Grandstand Section 18
Note: Walkway advisory in first 3 rows

Row	From Field	Row	From Field	Row	From Field
AA	15 Walk	BB	16 Walk	CC	17 Walk

DD	18 rows	HH	22 rows	MM	26 rows
EE	19 rows	JJ	23 rows	NN	27 rows
FF	20 rows	KK	24 rows		
GG	21 rows	LL	25 rows		

Loge Box 127

Rows: 13
Behind: Infield Dugout Boxes and Field Box 41
In front of: Grandstand Section 19
Note: Walkway advisory in first 3 rows

Row	From Field	Row	From Field	Row	From Field
A AA	15 Walk	FF	20 rows	LL	25 rows
BB	16 Walk	GG	21 rows	MM	26 rows
CC	17 Walk	HH	22 rows	NN	27 rows
DD	18 rows	JJ	23 rows		
EE	19 rows	KK	24 rows		

Loge Box 128

Rows: 13
Behind: Infield Dugout Boxes and Field Box 42
In front of: Grandstand Section 19
Note: Walkway advisory in first 3 rows

Row	From Field	Row	From Field	Row	From Field
AA	15 Walk	FF	20 rows	LL	25 rows
BB	16 Walk	GG	21 rows	MM	26 rows
CC	17 Walk	HH	22 rows	NN	27 rows
DD	18 rows	JJ	23 rows		
EE	19 rows	KK	24 rows		

Loge Box 129

Rows: 13
Behind: Infield Dugout Boxes and Field Box 43
In front of: Grandstand Section 20
Note: Loges Boxes 129-132 are directly behind home plate
Note: Walkway advisory in first 3 rows

Row	From Field	Row	From Field	Row	From Field
AA	15 Walk	FF	20 rows	LL	25 rows
BB	16 Walk	GG	21 rows	MM	26 rows
CC	17 Walk	HH	22 rows	NN	27 rows
DD	18 rows	JJ	23 rows		
EE	19 rows	KK	24 rows		

Loge Box 130

Rows: 13
Behind: Infield Dugout Boxes and Field Box 44
In front of: Grandstand Section 20
Note: Loges Boxes 129-132 are directly behind home plate
Note: Walkway advisory in first 3 rows

Row	From Field	Row	From Field	Row	From Field
AA	15 Walk	FF	20 rows	LL	25 rows
BB	16 Walk	GG	21 rows	MM	26 rows
CC	17 Walk	HH	22 rows	NN	27 rows
DD	18 rows	JJ	23 rows		
EE	19 rows	KK	24 rows		

Loge Box 131

Rows: 13
Behind: Infield Dugout Boxes and Field Box 45
In front of: Grandstand Section 21
Note: Loges Boxes 129-132 are directly behind home plate
Note: Walkway advisory in first 3 rows

Row	From Field	Row	From Field	Row	From Field
AA	15 Walk	FF	20 rows	LL	25 rows
BB	16 Walk	GG	21 rows	MM	26 rows
CC	17 Walk	HH	22 rows	NN	27 rows
DD	18 rows	JJ	23 rows		
EE	19 rows	KK	24 rows		

Loge Box 132

Rows: 13
Behind: Infield Dugout Boxes and Field Box 46
In front of: Grandstand Section 21
Note: Loges Boxes 129-132 are directly behind home plate
Note: Walkway advisory in first 3 rows

Row	From Field	Row	From Field	Row	From Field
AA	15 Walk	FF	20 rows	LL	25 rows
BB	16 Walk	GG	21 rows	MM	26 rows
CC	17 Walk	HH	22 rows	NN	27 rows
DD	18 rows	JJ	23 rows		
EE	19 rows	KK	24 rows		

Loge Box 133

Rows: 13
Behind: Infield Dugout Boxes and Field Box 47
In front of: Grandstand Section 22
Note: Walkway advisory in first 3 rows

Row	From Field	Row	From Field	Row	From Field
AA	15 Walk	FF	20 rows	LL	25 rows
BB	16 Walk	GG	21 rows	MM	26 rows
CC	17 Walk	HH	22 rows	NN	27 rows
DD	18 rows	JJ	23 rows		
EE	19 rows	KK	24 rows		

Loge Box 134

Rows: 13
Behind: Infield Dugout Boxes and Field Box 48
In front of: Grandstand Section 22
Note: Walkway advisory in first 3 rows

Row	From Field	Row	From Field	Row	From Field
AA	15 Walk	FF	20 rows	LL	25 rows
BB	16 Walk	GG	21 rows	MM	26 rows
CC	17 Walk	HH	22 rows	NN	27 rows
DD	18 rows	JJ	23 rows		
EE	19 rows	KK	24 rows		

Loge Box 135

Rows: 13
Behind: Infield Dugout Boxes and Field Box 49
In front of: Grandstand Section 23
Note: Walkway advisory in first 3 rows

Row	From Field	Row	From Field	Row	From Field
AA	15 Walk	FF	20 rows	LL	25 rows
BB	16 Walk	GG	21 rows	MM	26 rows
CC	17 Walk	HH	22 rows	NN	27 rows
DD	18 rows	JJ	23 rows		
EE	19 rows	KK	24 rows		

Loge Box 136

Rows: 13
Behind: Infield Dugout Boxes and Field Box 50
In front of: Grandstand Section 23
Note: Walkway advisory in first 3 rows

Row	From Field	Row	From Field	Row	From Field
AA	15 Walk	CC	17 Walk	EE	19 rows
BB	16 Walk	DD	18 rows	FF	20 rows

GG	21 rows	KK	24 rows	NN	27 rows
HH	22 rows	LL	25 rows		
JJ	23 rows	MM	26 rows		

Loge Box 137

Rows: 13
Behind: Infield Dugout Boxes and Field Box 51
In front of: Grandstand Section 24
Note: Walkway advisory in first 3 rows

Row	From Field	Row	From Field	Row	From Field
AA	15 Walk	FF	20 rows	LL	25 rows
BB	16 Walk	GG	21 rows	MM	26 rows
CC	17 Walk	HH	22 rows	NN	27 rows
DD	18 rows	JJ	23 rows		
EE	19 rows	KK	24 rows		

Loge Box 138

Rows: 13
Behind: Infield Dugout Boxes and Field Boxes 51and 52
In front of: Grandstand Section 24
Note: Walkway advisory in first 3 rows

Row	From Field	Row	From Field	Row	From Field
AA	15 Walk	FF	20 rows	LL	25 rows
BB	16 Walk	GG	21 rows	MM	26 rows
CC	17 Walk	HH	22 rows	NN	27 rows
DD	18 rows	JJ	23 rows		
EE	19 rows	KK	24 rows		

Loge Box 139

Rows: 13
Behind: Infield Dugout Boxes and Field Box 52
In front of: Grandstand Section 24
Note: Walkway advisory in first 3 rows

Row	From Field	Row	From Field	Row	From Field
AA	15 Walk	FF	20 rows	LL	25 rows
BB	16 Walk	GG	21 rows	MM	26 rows
CC	17 Walk	HH	22 rows	NN	27 rows
DD	18 rows	JJ	23 rows		
EE	19 rows	KK	24 rows		

Loge Box 140

Rows: 13
Behind: Infield Dugout Boxes and Field Box 53
In front of: Grandstand Section 24
Note: Walkway advisory in first 3 rows

Row	From Field	Row	From Field	Row	From Field
AA	15 Walk	FF	20 rows	LL	25 rows
BB	16 Walk	GG	21 rows	MM	26 rows
CC	17 Walk	HH	22 rows	NN	27 rows
DD	18 rows	JJ	23 rows		
EE	19 rows	KK	24 rows		

Loge Box 141

Rows: 13
Behind: Infield Dugout Boxes and Field Box 54
In front of: Grandstand Section 24
Note: Walkway advisory in first 3 rows

Row	From Field	Row	From Field	Row	From Field
AA	15 Walk	FF	20 rows	LL	25 rows
BB	16 Walk	GG	21 rows	MM	26 rows
CC	17 Walk	HH	22 rows	NN	27 rows
DD	18 rows	JJ	23 rows		
EE	19 rows	KK	24 rows		

Loge Box 142

Rows: 13
Behind: Infield Dugout Boxes and Field Box 55
In front of: Grandstand Section 25
Note: Walkway advisory in first 3 rows

Row	From Field	Row	From Field	Row	From Field
AA	15 Walk	FF	20 rows	LL	25 rows
BB	16 Walk	GG	21 rows	MM	26 rows
CC	17 Walk	HH	22 rows	NN	27 rows
DD	18 rows	JJ	23 rows		
EE	19 rows	KK	24 rows		

Loge Box 143

Rows: 13
Behind: Infield Dugout Boxes and Field Box 56
In front of: Grandstand Section 25
Note: Walkway advisory in first 3 rows

Row	From Field	Row	From Field	Row	From Field
AA	15 Walk	FF	20 rows	LL	25 rows
BB	16 Walk	GG	21 rows	MM	26 rows
CC	17 Walk	HH	22 rows	NN	27 rows
DD	18 rows	JJ	23 rows		
EE	19 rows	KK	24 rows		

Loge Box 144

Rows: 13
Behind: Infield Dugout Boxes and Field Box 57
In front of: Grandstand Section 25
Note: Walkway advisory in first 3 rows

Row	From Field	Row	From Field	Row	From Field
AA	15 Walk	FF	20 rows	LL	25 rows
BB	16 Walk	GG	21 rows	MM	26 rows
CC	17 Walk	HH	22 rows	NN	27 rows
DD	18 rows	JJ	23 rows		
EE	19 rows	KK	24 rows		

Loge Box 145

Rows: 13
Behind: Infield Dugout Boxes and Field Box 58
In front of: Grandstand Section 25
Note: Walkway advisory in first 3 rows

Row	From Field	Row	From Field	Row	From Field
AA	15 Walk	FF	20 rows	LL	25 rows
BB	16 Walk	GG	21 rows	MM	26 rows
CC	17 Walk	HH	22 rows	NN	27 rows
DD	18 rows	JJ	23 rows		
EE	19 rows	KK	24 rows		

Loge Box 146

Rows: 8
Behind: Infield Dugout Boxes and Field Box 60
In front of: Grandstand Section 25

Row	From Field	Row	From Field	Row	From Field
FF	20 rows	HH	22 rows	KK	24 rows
GG	21 rows	JJ	23 rows	LL	25 rows

MM	26 rows	NN	27 rows

Loge Box 147
Rows: 13
Behind: Infield Dugout Boxes and Field Box 61
In front of: Grandstand Section 26
Note: Walkway advisory in first 3 rows

Row	From Field	Row	From Field	Row	From Field
AA	15 Walk	FF	20 rows	LL	25 rows
BB	16 Walk	GG	21 rows	MM	26 rows
CC	17 Walk	HH	22 rows	NN	27 rows
DD	18 rows	JJ	23 rows		
EE	19 rows	KK	24 rows		

Loge Box 148
Rows: 13
Behind: 3rd base dugout and Field Box 62
In front of: Grandstand Section 26
Note: Walkway advisory in first 3 rows

Row	From Field	Row	From Field	Row	From Field
AA	11 Walk	FF	16 rows	LL	21 rows
BB	12 Walk	GG	17 rows	MM	22 rows
CC	13 Walk	HH	18 rows	NN	23 rows
DD	14 rows	JJ	19 rows		
EE	15 rows	KK	20 rows		

Loge Box 149
Rows: 13
Behind: 3rd base dugout and Field Boxes 63 and 64
In front of: Grandstand Section 26
Note: Walkway advisory in first 3 rows

Row	From Field	Row	From Field	Row	From Field
AA	11 Walk	FF	16 rows	LL	21 rows
BB	12 Walk	GG	17 rows	MM	22 rows
CC	13 Walk	HH	18 rows	NN	23 rows
DD	14 rows	JJ	19 rows		
EE	15 rows	KK	20 rows		

Loge Box 150

Rows: 13
Behind: 3rd base dugout and Field Boxes 64 and 65
In front of: Grandstand Section 26
Note: Walkway advisory in first 3 rows

Row	From Field	Row	From Field	Row	From Field
AA	11 Walk	FF	16 rows	LL	21 rows
BB	12 Walk	GG	17 rows	MM	22 rows
CC	13 Walk	HH	18 rows	NN	23 rows
DD	14 rows	JJ	19 rows		
EE	15 rows	KK	20 rows		

Loge Box 151

Rows: 13
Behind: 3rd base dugout and Field Box 66
In front of: Grandstand Section 27

Row	From Field	Row	From Field	Row	From Field
AA	11 Walk	FF	16 rows	LL	21 rows
BB	12 Walk	GG	17 rows	MM	22 rows
CC	13 Walk	HH	18 rows	NN	23 rows
DD	14 rows	JJ	19 rows		
EE	15 rows	KK	20 rows		

Loge Box 152

Rows: 13
Behind: 3rd base dugout and Field Box 67
In front of: Grandstand Section 27
Note: Walkway advisory in first 3 rows

Row	From Field	Row	From Field	Row	From Field
AA	11 Walk	FF	16 rows	LL	21 rows
BB	12 Walk	GG	17 rows	MM	22 rows
CC	13 Walk	HH	18 rows	NN	23 rows
DD	14 rows	JJ	19 rows		
EE	15 rows	KK	20 rows		

Loge Box 153

Rows: 13
Behind: 3rd base dugout and Field Box 68
In front of: Grandstand Section 27
Note: Walkway advisory in first 3 rows

Row	From Field	Row	From Field	Row	From Field
AA	11 Walk	CC	13 Walk	EE	15 rows
BB	12 Walk	DD	14 rows	FF	16 rows

GG	17 rows	KK	20 rows	NN	24 rows
HH	18 rows	LL	21 rows		
JJ	19 rows	MM	23 rows		

Loge Box 154

Rows: 13
Behind: Field Box 69
In front of: Grandstand Section 27
Note: Walkway advisory in first 3 rows

Row	From Field	Row	From Field	Row	From Field
AA	13 Walk	FF	18 rows	LL	23 rows
BB	14 Walk	GG	19 rows	MM	24 rows
CC	15 Walk	HH	20 rows	NN	25 rows
DD	16 rows	JJ	21 rows		
EE	17 rows	KK	22 rows		

Loge Box 155

Rows: 13
Behind: Field Box 70
In front of: Grandstand Section 27
Note: Walkway advisory in first 3 rows

Row	From Field	Row	From Field	Row	From Field
AA	13 Walk	FF	18 rows	LL	23 rows
BB	14 Walk	GG	19 rows	MM	24 rows
CC	15 Walk	HH	20 rows	NN	25 rows
DD	16 rows	JJ	21 rows		
EE	17 rows	KK	22 rows		

Loge Box 156

Rows: 12
Behind: Field Box 70
In front of: Grandstand Section 29
Note: Walkway advisory in first 3 rows

Row	From Field	Row	From Field	Row	From Field
AA	13 Walk	EE	17 rows	JJ	21 rows
BB	14 Walk	FF	18 rows	KK	22 rows
CC	15 Walk	GG	19 rows	LL	23 rows
DD	16 rows	HH	20 rows	MM	24 rows

Loge Box 157

Rows: 12
Behind: Field Box 71
In front of: Grandstand Section 29
Note: Walkway advisory in first 3 rows

Row	From Field	Row	From Field	Row	From Field
AA	12 Walk	EE	16 rows	JJ	20 rows
BB	13 Walk	FF	17 rows	KK	21 rows
CC	14 Walk	GG	18 rows	LL	22 rows
DD	15 rows	HH	19 rows	MM	23 rows

Loge Box 158

Rows: 12
Behind: Field Box 71
In front of: Grandstand Sections 29 and 30
Note: Walkway advisory in first 3 rows

Row	From Field	Row	From Field	Row	From Field
AA	11 Walk	EE	15 rows	JJ	19 rows
BB	12 Walk	FF	16 rows	KK	20 rows
CC	13 Walk	GG	17 rows	LL	21 rows
DD	14 rows	HH	18 rows	MM	22 rows

Loge Box 159

Rows: 13
Behind: Extended Dugout Boxes and Field Boxes 72, 73 and 74
In front of: Grandstand Section 30
Note: Walkway advisory in first 2 rows

Row	From Field	Row	From Field	Row	From Field
BB	15 Walk	GG	20 rows	MM	25 rows
CC	16 Walk	HH	21 rows	NN	26 rows
DD	17 rows	JJ	22 rows	PP	27 rows
EE	18 rows	KK	23 rows		
FF	19 rows	LL	24 rows		

Loge Box 160

Rows: 14
Behind: Extended Dugout Boxes and Field Boxes 75, 76, and 77
In front of: Grandstand Section 30

Row	From Field	Row	From Field	Row	From Field
AA	14 rows	FF	19 rows	LL	24 rows
BB	15 rows	GG	20 rows	MM	25 rows
CC	16 rows	HH	21 rows	NN	26 rows
DD	17 rows	JJ	22 rows	PP	27 rows
EE	18 rows	KK	23 rows		

Loge Box 161

Rows: 14
Behind: Extended Dugout Boxes and Field Boxes 78, 79, and 80
In front of: Grandstand Section 31

Row	From Field	Row	From Field	Row	From Field
AA	14 rows	FF	19 rows	LL	24 rows
BB	15 rows	GG	20 rows	MM	25 rows
CC	16 rows	HH	21 rows	NN	26 rows
DD	17 rows	JJ	22 rows	PP	27 rows
EE	18 rows	KK	23 rows		

Loge Box 162

Rows: 12
Behind: Field Boxes 81 and 82
In front of: Grandstand Section 31

Row	From Field	Row	From Field	Row	From Field
AA	10 rows	EE	14 rows	JJ	18 rows
BB	11 rows	FF	15 rows	KK	19 rows
CC	12 rows	GG	16 rows	LL	20 rows
DD	13 rows	HH	17 rows	MM	21 rows

Loge Box 163

Rows: 14
Behind: Partially on the field and partially behind Field Box 82
In front of: Grandstand Section 32

Row	From Field	Row	From Field	Row	From Field
AA	2 rows	FF	7 rows	LL	12 rows
BB	3 rows	GG	8 rows	MM	13 rows
CC	4 rows	HH	9 rows	NN	14 rows
DD	5 rows	JJ	10 rows	PP	15 rows
EE	6 rows	KK	11 rows		

Loge Box 164

Rows: 14
Behind: This box is on the field
In front of: Grandstand Section 32

Row	From Field	Row	From Field	Row	From Field
AA	on the field	FF	6 rows	LL	11 rows
BB	2 rows	GG	7 rows	MM	12 rows
CC	3 rows	HH	8 rows	NN	13 rows
DD	4 rows	JJ	9 rows	PP	14 rows
EE	5 rows	KK	10 rows		

Loge Box 165
Rows: 6
Behind: This box is on the field
In front of: Grandstand Section 33

Row	From Field	Row	From Field	Row	From Field
JJ	on the field	LL	3 rows	NN	5 rows
KK	2 rows	MM	4 rows	PP	6 rows

Field Boxes

The Field Box sections extend from just past first base with Box 9 all the way around the infield to Box 82, which is on the short wall halfway between third base and the Green Monster. Most of the Field Box sections are behind two rows of Dugout Box Seats or one of the dugouts. See details below.

Field Box 9
Rows: 12
Behind: Handicapped Extended Dugout Boxes
In front of: Loge Box 98

Row	From Field	Row	From Field	Row	From Field
A	3 rows	E	7 rows	J	11 rows
B	4 rows	F	8 rows	K	12 rows
C	5 rows	G	9 rows	L	13 rows
D	6 rows	H	10 rows	M	14 rows

Field Box 10
Rows: 12
Behind: Extended Dugout Boxes
In front of: Loge Box 99

Row	From Field	Row	From Field	Row	From Field
A	3 rows	E	7 rows	J	11 rows
B	4 rows	F	8 rows	K	12 rows
C	5 rows	G	9 rows	L	13 rows
D	6 rows	H	10 rows	M	14 rows

Field Box 11

Rows: 12
Behind: Extended Dugout Boxes
In front of: Loge Box 100

Row	From Field	Row	From Field	Row	From Field
A	3 rows	E	7 rows	J	11 rows
B	4 rows	F	8 rows	K	12 rows
C	5 rows	G	9 rows	L	13 rows
D	6 rows	H	10 rows	M	14 rows

Field Box 12

Rows: 11
Behind: Extended Dugout Boxes
In front of: Loge Box 100

Row	From Field	Row	From Field	Row	From Field
A	3 rows	E	7 rows	J	11 rows
B	4 rows	F	8 rows	K	12 rows
C	5 rows	G	9 rows	L	13 rows
D	6 rows	H	10 rows		

Field Box 13

Rows: 11
Behind: Extended Dugout Boxes
In front of: Loge Box 101

Row	From Field	Row	From Field	Row	From Field
A	3 rows	E	7 rows	J	11 rows
B	4 rows	F	8 rows	K	12 rows
C	5 rows	G	9 rows	L	13 rows
D	6 rows	H	10 rows		

Field Box 14

Rows: 12
Behind: Extended Dugout Boxes
In front of: Loge Box 102

Row	From Field	Row	From Field	Row	From Field
A	3 rows	E	7 rows	J	11 rows
B	4 rows	F	8 rows	K	12 rows
C	5 rows	G	9 rows	L	13 rows
D	6 rows	H	10 rows	M	14 rows

Field Box 15
Rows: 12
Behind: Extended Dugout Boxes
In front of: Loge Box 102

Row	From Field	Row	From Field	Row	From Field
A	3 rows	E	7 rows	J	11 rows
B	4 rows	F	8 rows	K	12 rows
C	5 rows	G	9 rows	L	13 rows
D	6 rows	H	10 rows	M	14 rows

Field Box 16
Rows: 12
Behind: Extended Dugout Boxes
In front of: Loge Box 103

Row	From Field	Row	From Field	Row	From Field
A	3 rows	E	7 rows	J	11 rows
B	4 rows	F	8 rows	K	12 rows
C	5 rows	G	9 rows	L	13 rows
D	6 rows	H	10 rows	M	14 rows

Field Box 17
Rows: 12
Behind: Photographer's well
In front of: Loge Box 104

Row	From Field	Row	From Field	Row	From Field
A	on the field	E	5 rows	J	9 rows
B	2 rows	F	6 rows	K	10 rows
C	3 rows	G	7 rows	L	11 rows
D	4 rows	H	8 rows	M	12 rows

Field Box 18
Rows: 12
Behind: Photographer's well
In front of: Loge Box 105

Row	From Field	Row	From Field	Row	From Field
A	on the field	E	5 rows	J	9 rows
B	2 rows	F	6 rows	K	10 rows
C	3 rows	G	7 rows	L	11 rows
D	4 rows	H	8 rows	M	12 rows

Field Box 19
Rows: 12
Behind: Photographer's well
In front of: Loge Box 106

Row	From Field	Row	From Field	Row	From Field
A	on the field	E	5 rows	J	9 rows
B	2 rows	F	6 rows	K	10 rows
C	3 rows	G	7 rows	L	11 rows
D	4 rows	H	8 rows	M	12 rows

Field Box 20
Rows: 12
Behind: Photographer's well
In front of: Loge Box 107

Row	From Field	Row	From Field	Row	From Field
A	on the field	E	5 rows	J	9 rows
B	2 rows	F	6 rows	K	10 rows
C	3 rows	G	7 rows	L	11 rows
D	4 rows	H	8 rows	M	12 rows

Field Box 21
Rows: 10
Behind: Red Sox dugout
In front of: Loge Box 108

Row	From Field	Row	From Field	Row	From Field
C	on the field	G	5 rows	L	9 rows
D	2 rows	H	6 rows	M	10 rows
E	3 rows	J	7 rows		
F	4 rows	K	8 rows		

Field Box 22
Rows: 10
Behind: Red Sox dugout
In front of: Loge Box 109

Row	From Field	Row	From Field	Row	From Field
C	on the field	G	5 rows	L	9 rows
D	2 rows	H	6 rows	M	10 rows
E	3 rows	J	7 rows		
F	4 rows	K	8 rows		

Field Box 23

Rows: 10
Behind: Red Sox dugout
In front of: Loge Box 110

Row	From Field	Row	From Field	Row	From Field
C	on the field	G	5 rows	L	9 rows
D	2 rows	H	6 rows	M	10 rows
E	3 rows	J	7 rows		
F	4 rows	K	8 rows		

Field Box 24

Rows: 10
Behind: Red Sox dugout
In front of: Loge Box 111

Row	From Field	Row	From Field	Row	From Field
C	on the field	G	5 rows	L	9 rows
D	2 rows	H	6 rows	M	10 rows
E	3 rows	J	7 rows		
F	4 rows	K	8 rows		

Field Box 25

Rows: 10
Behind: Red Sox dugout
In front of: Loge Box 112

Row	From Field	Row	From Field	Row	From Field
C	on the field	G	5 rows	L	9 rows
D	2 rows	H	6 rows	M	10 rows
E	3 rows	J	7 rows		
F	4 rows	K	8 rows		

Field Box 26

Rows: 10
Behind: Red Sox dugout
In front of: Loge Box 113

Row	From Field	Row	From Field	Row	From Field
C	on the field	G	5 rows	L	9 rows
D	2 rows	H	6 rows	M	10 rows
E	3 rows	J	7 rows		
F	4 rows	K	8 rows		

Field Box 27
Rows: 10
Behind: Red Sox dugout
In front of: Loge Box 114

Row	From Field	Row	From Field	Row	From Field
C	on the field	G	5 rows	L	9 rows
D	2 rows	H	6 rows	M	10 rows
E	3 rows	J	7 rows		
F	4 rows	K	8 rows		

Field Box 28
Rows: 10
Behind: Red Sox dugout
In front of: Loge Boxes 114 and 115

Row	From Field	Row	From Field	Row	From Field
C	on the field	G	5 rows	L	9 rows
D	2 rows	H	6 rows	M	10 rows
E	3 rows	J	7 rows		
F	4 rows	K	8 rows		

Field Box 29
Rows: 12
Behind: Dugout Boxes
In front of: Loge Boxes 115 and 116

Row	From Field	Row	From Field	Row	From Field
A	3 rows	E	7 rows	J	11 rows
B	4 rows	F	8 rows	K	12 rows
C	5 rows	G	9 rows	L	13 rows
D	6 rows	H	10 rows	M	14 rows

Field Box 30
Rows: 12
Behind: Dugout Boxes
In front of: Loge Box 116

Row	From Field	Row	From Field	Row	From Field
A	3 rows	E	7 rows	J	11 rows
B	4 rows	F	8 rows	K	12 rows
C	5 rows	G	9 rows	L	13 rows
D	6 rows	H	10 rows	M	14 rows

Field Box 31

Rows: 12
Behind: Dugout Boxes
In front of: Loge Box 117

Row	From Field	Row	From Field	Row	From Field
A	3 rows	E	7 rows	J	11 rows
B	4 rows	F	8 rows	K	12 rows
C	5 rows	G	9 rows	L	13 rows
D	6 rows	H	10 rows	M	14 rows

Field Box 32

Rows: 12
Behind: Dugout Boxes
In front of: Loge Box 118

Row	From Field	Row	From Field	Row	From Field
A	3 rows	E	7 rows	J	11 rows
B	4 rows	F	8 rows	K	12 rows
C	5 rows	G	9 rows	L	13 rows
D	6 rows	H	10 rows	M	14 rows

Field Box 33

Rows: 12
Behind: Dugout Boxes
In front of: Loge Box 119

Row	From Field	Row	From Field	Row	From Field
A	3 rows	E	7 rows	J	11 rows
B	4 rows	F	8 rows	K	12 rows
C	5 rows	G	9 rows	L	13 rows
D	6 rows	H	10 rows	M	14 rows

Field Box 34

Rows: 12
Behind: Dugout Boxes
In front of: Loge Box 120

Row	From Field	Row	From Field	Row	From Field
A	3 rows	E	7 rows	J	11 rows
B	4 rows	F	8 rows	K	12 rows
C	5 rows	G	9 rows	L	13 rows
D	6 rows	H	10 rows	M	14 rows

Field Box 35

Rows: 12
Behind: Dugout Boxes
In front of: Loge Boxes 120 and 121

Row	From Field	Row	From Field	Row	From Field
A	3 rows	E	7 rows	J	11 rows
B	4 rows	F	8 rows	K	12 rows
C	5 rows	G	9 rows	L	13 rows
D	6 rows	H	10 rows	M	14 rows

Field Box 36

Rows: 12
Behind: Dugout Boxes
In front of: Loge Box 121

Row	From Field	Row	From Field	Row	From Field
A	3 rows	E	7 rows	J	11 rows
B	4 rows	F	8 rows	K	12 rows
C	5 rows	G	9 rows	L	13 rows
D	6 rows	H	10 rows	M	14 rows

Field Box 37

Rows: 12
Behind: Dugout Boxes
In front of: Loge Box 122

Row	From Field	Row	From Field	Row	From Field
A	3 rows	E	7 rows	J	11 rows
B	4 rows	F	8 rows	K	12 rows
C	5 rows	G	9 rows	L	13 rows
D	6 rows	H	10 rows	M	14 rows

Field Box 38

Rows: 12
Behind: Dugout Boxes
In front of: Loge Boxes 123 and 124

Row	From Field	Row	From Field	Row	From Field
A	3 rows	E	7 rows	J	11 rows
B	4 rows	F	8 rows	K	12 rows
C	5 rows	G	9 rows	L	13 rows
D	6 rows	H	10 rows	M	14 rows

Field Box 39

Rows: 12
Behind: Dugout Boxes
In front of: Loge Box 125

Row	From Field	Row	From Field	Row	From Field
A	3 rows	E	7 rows	J	11 rows
B	4 rows	F	8 rows	K	12 rows
C	5 rows	G	9 rows	L	13 rows
D	6 rows	H	10 rows	M	14 rows

Field Box 40

Rows: 12
Behind: Dugout Boxes and backstop screen
In front of: Loge Box 126

Row	From Field	Row	From Field	Row	From Field
A	3 rows	E	7 rows	J	11 rows
B	4 rows	F	8 rows	K	12 rows
C	5 rows	G	9 rows	L	13 rows
D	6 rows	H	10 rows	M	14 rows

Field Box 41

Rows: 12
Behind: Dugout Boxes and backstop screen
In front of: Loge Box 127

Row	From Field	Row	From Field	Row	From Field
A	3 rows	E	7 rows	J	11 rows
B	4 rows	F	8 rows	K	12 rows
C	5 rows	G	9 rows	L	13 rows
D	6 rows	H	10 rows	M	14 rows

Field Box 42

Rows: 12
Behind: Dugout Boxes and backstop screen
In front of: Loge Box 128

Row	From Field	Row	From Field	Row	From Field
A	3 rows	E	7 rows	J	11 rows
B	4 rows	F	8 rows	K	12 rows
C	5 rows	G	9 rows	L	13 rows
D	6 rows	H	10 rows	M	14 rows

Field Box 43

Rows: 12
Behind: Dugout Boxes and backstop screen
In front of: Loge Box 129

Row	From Field	Row	From Field	Row	From Field
A	3 rows	E	7 rows	J	11 rows
B	4 rows	F	8 rows	K	12 rows
C	5 rows	G	9 rows	L	13 rows
D	6 rows	H	10 rows	M	14 rows

Field Box 44

Rows: 12
Behind: Dugout Boxes and backstop screen
In front of: Loge Box 130

Row	From Field	Row	From Field	Row	From Field
A	3 rows	E	7 rows	J	11 rows
B	4 rows	F	8 rows	K	12 rows
C	5 rows	G	9 rows	L	13 rows
D	6 rows	H	10 rows	M	14 rows

Field Box 45

Rows: 12
Behind: Dugout Boxes and backstop screen
In front of: Loge Box 131

Row	From Field	Row	From Field	Row	From Field
A	3 rows	E	7 rows	J	11 rows
B	4 rows	F	8 rows	K	12 rows
C	5 rows	G	9 rows	L	13 rows
D	6 rows	H	10 rows	M	14 rows

Field Box 46

Rows: 12
Behind: Dugout Boxes and backstop screen
In front of: Loge Box 132

Row	From Field	Row	From Field	Row	From Field
A	3 rows	E	7 rows	J	11 rows
B	4 rows	F	8 rows	K	12 rows
C	5 rows	G	9 rows	L	13 rows
D	6 rows	H	10 rows	M	14 rows

Field Box 47

Rows: 12
Behind: Dugout Boxes and backstop screen
In front of: Loge Box 133

Row	From Field	Row	From Field	Row	From Field
A	3 rows	E	7 rows	J	11 rows
B	4 rows	F	8 rows	K	12 rows
C	5 rows	G	9 rows	L	13 rows
D	6 rows	H	10 rows	M	14 rows

Field Box 48

Rows: 12
Behind: Dugout Boxes and backstop screen
In front of: Loge Box 134

Row	From Field	Row	From Field	Row	From Field
A	3 rows	E	7 rows	J	11 rows
B	4 rows	F	8 rows	K	12 rows
C	5 rows	G	9 rows	L	13 rows
D	6 rows	H	10 rows	M	14 rows

Field Box 49

Rows: 12
Behind: Dugout Boxes and backstop screen
In front of: Loge Box 135

Row	From Field	Row	From Field	Row	From Field
A	3 rows	E	7 rows	J	11 rows
B	4 rows	F	8 rows	K	12 rows
C	5 rows	G	9 rows	L	13 rows
D	6 rows	H	10 rows	M	14 rows

Field Box 50

Rows: 12
Behind: Dugout Boxes
In front of: Loge Box 136

Row	From Field	Row	From Field	Row	From Field
A	3 rows	E	7 rows	J	11 rows
B	4 rows	F	8 rows	K	12 rows
C	5 rows	G	9 rows	L	13 rows
D	6 rows	H	10 rows	M	14 rows

Field Box 51

Rows: 12
Behind: Dugout Boxes
In front of: Loge Boxes 137 and 138

Row	From Field	Row	From Field	Row	From Field
A	3 rows	E	7 rows	J	11 rows
B	4 rows	F	8 rows	K	12 rows
C	5 rows	G	9 rows	L	13 rows
D	6 rows	H	10 rows	M	14 rows

Field Box 52

Rows: 12
Behind: Dugout Boxes
In front of: Loge Box 139

Row	From Field	Row	From Field	Row	From Field
A	3 rows	E	7 rows	J	11 rows
B	4 rows	F	8 rows	K	12 rows
C	5 rows	G	9 rows	L	13 rows
D	6 rows	H	10 rows	M	14 rows

Field Box 53

Rows: 12
Behind: Dugout Boxes
In front of: Loge Box 140

Row	From Field	Row	From Field	Row	From Field
A	3 rows	E	7 rows	J	11 rows
B	4 rows	F	8 rows	K	12 rows
C	5 rows	G	9 rows	L	13 rows
D	6 rows	H	10 rows	M	14 rows

Field Box 54

Rows: 12
Behind: Dugout Boxes
In front of: Loge Box 141

Row	From Field	Row	From Field	Row	From Field
A	3 rows	E	7 rows	J	11 rows
B	4 rows	F	8 rows	K	12 rows
C	5 rows	G	9 rows	L	13 rows
D	6 rows	H	10 rows	M	14 rows

Field Box 55
Rows: 12
Behind: Dugout Boxes
In front of: Loge Box 142

Row	From Field	Row	From Field	Row	From Field
A	3 rows	E	7 rows	J	11 rows
B	4 rows	F	8 rows	K	12 rows
C	5 rows	G	9 rows	L	13 rows
D	6 rows	H	10 rows	M	14 rows

Field Box 56
Rows: 12
Behind: Dugout Boxes
In front of: Loge Box 143

Row	From Field	Row	From Field	Row	From Field
A	3 rows	E	7 rows	J	11 rows
B	4 rows	F	8 rows	K	12 rows
C	5 rows	G	9 rows	L	13 rows
D	6 rows	H	10 rows	M	14 rows

Field Box 57
Rows: 12
Behind: Dugout Boxes
In front of: Loge Box 144

Row	From Field	Row	From Field	Row	From Field
A	3 rows	E	7 rows	J	11 rows
B	4 rows	F	8 rows	K	12 rows
C	5 rows	G	9 rows	L	13 rows
D	6 rows	H	10 rows	M	14 rows

Field Box 58
Rows: 12
Behind: Dugout Boxes
In front of: Loge Box 145

Row	From Field	Row	From Field	Row	From Field
A	3 rows	E	7 rows	J	11 rows
B	4 rows	F	8 rows	K	12 rows
C	5 rows	G	9 rows	L	13 rows
D	6 rows	H	10 rows	M	14 rows

Field Box 59

Rows: 12
Behind: Dugout Boxes
In front of: Loge Box 145

Row	From Field	Row	From Field	Row	From Field
A	3 rows	E	7 rows	J	11 rows
B	4 rows	F	8 rows	K	12 rows
C	5 rows	G	9 rows	L	13 rows
D	6 rows	H	10 rows	M	14 rows

Field Box 60

Rows: 12
Behind: Dugout Boxes
In front of: Loge Box 146

Row	From Field	Row	From Field	Row	From Field
A	3 rows	E	7 rows	J	11 rows
B	4 rows	F	8 rows	K	12 rows
C	5 rows	G	9 rows	L	13 rows
D	6 rows	H	10 rows	M	14 rows

Field Box 61

Rows: 12
Behind: Dugout Boxes
In front of: Loge Box 147

Row	From Field	Row	From Field	Row	From Field
A	3 rows	E	7 rows	J	11 rows
B	4 rows	F	8 rows	K	12 rows
C	5 rows	G	9 rows	L	13 rows
D	6 rows	H	10 rows	M	14 rows

Field Box 62

Rows: 10
Behind: 3rd base dugout
In front of: Loge Box 148

Row	From Field	Row	From Field	Row	From Field
C	on the field	G	5 rows	L	9 rows
D	2 rows	H	6 rows	M	10 rows
E	3 rows	J	7 rows		
F	4 rows	K	8 rows		

Field Box 63

Rows: 10
Behind: 3rd base dugout
In front of: Loge Box 149

Row	From Field	Row	From Field	Row	From Field
C	on the field	G	5 rows	L	9 rows
D	2 rows	H	6 rows	M	10 rows
E	3 rows	J	7 rows		
F	4 rows	K	8 rows		

Field Box 64

Rows: 10
Behind: 3rd base dugout
In front of: Loge Box 149

Row	From Field	Row	From Field	Row	From Field
C	on the field	G	5 rows	L	9 rows
D	2 rows	H	6 rows	M	10 rows
E	3 rows	J	7 rows		
F	4 rows	K	8 rows		

Field Box 65

Rows: 10
Behind: 3rd base dugout
In front of: Loge Box 150

Row	From Field	Row	From Field	Row	From Field
C	on the field	G	5 rows	L	9 rows
D	2 rows	H	6 rows	M	10 rows
E	3 rows	J	7 rows		
F	4 rows	K	8 rows		

Field Box 66

Rows: 10
Behind: 3rd base dugout
In front of: Loge Boxes 150 and 151

Row	From Field	Row	From Field	Row	From Field
C	on the field	G	5 rows	L	9 rows
D	2 rows	H	6 rows	M	10 rows
E	3 rows	J	7 rows		
F	4 rows	K	8 rows		

Field Box 67

Rows: 10
Behind: 3rd base dugout
In front of: Loge Boxes 151 and 152

Row	From Field	Row	From Field	Row	From Field
C	on the field	G	5 rows	L	9 rows
D	2 rows	H	6 rows	M	10 rows
E	3 rows	J	7 rows		
F	4 rows	K	8 rows		

Field Box 68

Rows: 10
Behind: 3rd base dugout
In front of: Loge Boxes 153 and 154

Row	From Field	Row	From Field	Row	From Field
C	on the field	G	5 rows	L	9 rows
D	2 rows	H	6 rows	M	10 rows
E	3 rows	J	7 rows		
F	4 rows	K	8 rows		

Field Box 69

Rows: 12
Behind: Photographer's well
In front of: Loge Box 155

Row	From Field	Row	From Field	Row	From Field
A	on the field	E	5 rows	J	9 rows
B	2 rows	F	6 rows	K	10 rows
C	3 rows	G	7 rows	L	11 rows
D	4 rows	H	8 rows	M	12 rows

Field Box 70

Rows: 12
Behind: Photographer's well
In front of: Loge Boxes 155 and 156

Row	From Field	Row	From Field	Row	From Field
A	on the field	E	5 rows	J	9 rows
B	2 rows	F	6 rows	K	10 rows
C	3 rows	G	7 rows	L	11 rows
D	4 rows	H	8 rows	M	12 rows

Field Box 71

Rows: 11
Behind: Photographer's well
In front of: Loge Boxes 157 and 158

Row	From Field	Row	From Field	Row	From Field
A	on the field	E	5 rows	J	9 rows
B	2 rows	F	6 rows	K	10 rows
C	3 rows	G	7 rows	L	11 rows
D	4 rows	H	8 rows		

Field Box 72

Rows: 11
Behind: Extended Dugout Boxes
In front of: Loge Box 159

Row	From Field	Row	From Field	Row	From Field
A	3 rows	E	7 rows	J	11 rows
B	4 rows	F	8 rows	K	12 rows
C	5 rows	G	9 rows	L	13 rows
D	6 rows	H	10 rows		

Field Box 73

Rows: 11
Behind: Extended Dugout Boxes
In front of: Loge Box 159

Row	From Field	Row	From Field	Row	From Field
A	3 rows	E	7 rows	J	11 rows
B	4 rows	F	8 rows	K	12 rows
C	5 rows	G	9 rows	L	13 rows
D	6 rows	H	10 rows		

Field Box 74

Rows: 11
Behind: Extended Dugout Boxes
In front of: Loge Box 159

Row	From Field	Row	From Field	Row	From Field
A	3 rows	E	7 rows	J	11 rows
B	4 rows	F	8 rows	K	12 rows
C	5 rows	G	9 rows	L	13 rows
D	6 rows	H	10 rows		

Field Box 75

Rows: 11
Behind: Extended Dugout Boxes
In front of: Loge Box 160

Row	From Field	Row	From Field	Row	From Field
A	3 rows	E	7 rows	J	11 rows
B	4 rows	F	8 rows	K	12 rows
C	5 rows	G	9 rows	L	13 rows
D	6 rows	H	10 rows		

Field Box 76

Rows: 11
Behind: Extended Dugout Boxes
In front of: Loge Box 160

Row	From Field	Row	From Field	Row	From Field
A	3 rows	E	7 rows	J	11 rows
B	4 rows	F	8 rows	K	12 rows
C	5 rows	G	9 rows	L	13 rows
D	6 rows	H	10 rows		

Field Box 77

Rows: 11
Behind: Extended Dugout Boxes
In front of: Loge Box 160

Row	From Field	Row	From Field	Row	From Field
A	3 rows	E	7 rows	J	11 rows
B	4 rows	F	8 rows	K	12 rows
C	5 rows	G	9 rows	L	13 rows
D	6 rows	H	10 rows		

Field Box 78

Rows: 11
Behind: Extended Dugout Boxes
In front of: Loge Box 161

Row	From Field	Row	From Field	Row	From Field
A	3 rows	E	7 rows	J	11 rows
B	4 rows	F	8 rows	K	12 rows
C	5 rows	G	9 rows	L	13 rows
D	6 rows	H	10 rows		

Field Box 79

Rows: 11
Behind: Extended Dugout Boxes
In front of: Loge Box 161

Row	From Field	Row	From Field	Row	From Field
A	3 rows	E	7 rows	J	11 rows
B	4 rows	F	8 rows	K	12 rows
C	5 rows	G	9 rows	L	13 rows
D	6 rows	H	10 rows		

Field Box 80

Rows: 11
Behind: Extended Dugout Boxes
In front of: Loge Box 161

Row	From Field	Row	From Field	Row	From Field
A	2 rows	E	6 rows	J	10 rows
B	3 rows	F	7 rows	K	11 rows
C	4 rows	G	8 rows	L	12 rows
D	5 rows	H	9 rows		

Field Box 81

Rows: 10
Behind: This box is on the field
In front of: Loge Box 162

Row	From Field	Row	From Field	Row	From Field
B	on the field	F	5 rows	K	9 rows
C	2 rows	G	6 rows	L	10 rows
D	3 rows	H	7 rows		
E	4 rows	J	8 rows		

Field Box 82

Rows: 8
Behind: This box is on the field
In front of: Loge Boxes 162 and 163
Note: This is a triangular box located on the wall between third base and the Green Monster. The last seat in each row is on the field.

Row	From Field	Row	From Field	Row	From Field
B	on the field	F	5 rows	K	9 rows
C	2 rows	G	6 rows	L	10 rows
D	3 rows	H	7 rows		
E	4 rows	J	8 rows		

Grandstand

Unlike the Field Box and Loge Box sections, the rows in the Grandstand sections are identified with numerals, rather than letters or double letters, so it is much easier to determine where your row is within your section. But where is your row in relation to the field? To determine this, add the number of your row to the number listed below for each section. For example, if you are sitting in Grandstand Section 24, row 11, you should add 27 to 11, so you will be 38 rows from the field.

Section 1
Add 31 to your row number

Section 2
Add 31 to your row number

Section 3
Add 31 to your row number

Section 4
Add 31 to your row number

Section 5
Add 31 to your row number

Section 6
Add 30 to your row number

Section 7
Add 27 to your row number

Section 8
Add 29 to your row number

Section 9
Add 34 to your row number

Section 10
Add 34 to your row number

Section 11
Add 30 to your row number

Section 12
Add 30 to your row number

Section 13
Add 28 to your row number

Section 14
Add 23 to your row number

Section 15
Add 23 to your row number

Section 16
Add 27 to your row number

Section 17
Add 27 to your row number

Section 18
Add 27 to your row number

Section 19
Add 27 to your row number

Section 20
Add 27 to your row number
Section 21
Add 27 to your row number

Section 22
Add 27 to your row number

Section 23
Add 27 to your row number

Section 24
Add 27 to your row number

Section 25
Add 27 to your row number

Section 26
Add 24 to your row number
Section 27
Add 24 to your row number

Section 29
Add 24 to your row number
Section 30
Add 30 to your row number

Section 31
Add 21 to 27, it varies

Section 32
Add 8 to 14, it varies

Section 33
Add 1 to 6, it varies

The Bleachers

Most of the bleacher sections are either on the field or behind the bullpens, with the exception of Sections 37, 38 and 39. So if Row 1 of a section is on the field (or behind a bullpen), then Row 12 is 12 rows off the field, and so on. See details below.

Section 34

A small section just to the left of the Green Monster and the centerfield television cameras, Section 34 gives you the same view of home plate as the centerfielder.

There are 9 rows in this section, with Row 1 on the field, Row 2 is two rows off the field, and so on.

Section 35

This section is in dead centerfield. If you want to be able to call balls and strikes over the pitcher's shoulder, get seats 1 or 2 in any of the rows.

There are 18 rows in this section, with Row 1 on the field, Row 2 is two rows off the field, and so on.

Section 36

This section is just to the right of center field and is near the warning track triangle. It is also above the Bleacher Bar, which opened in 2008.

There are 30 rows in this section, with Row 1 on the field, Row 2 is two rows off the field, and so on.

Section 37

In typically quirky Fenway fashion, the rows in Section 37 (and 38) face the right field foul line. This is one of three bleacher sections that is not directly on either the field or behind a bullpen.

There are 40 rows in this section. The first few seats in Row 1 are on the field (just above the point of the warning track triangle), but the rest of the seats are behind Section 40 and the Red Sox bullpen. To determine how far your seats are from the field, add approximately 5 rows to your row number, for example, Row 10 is about 15 rows off the field.

Section 38

Like Section 37, this section's rows face the right field foul line. It is a triangular section, tucked in between sections 37 and 39, and behind Section 40.

There are 40 rows in this section, with between 5 and 28 seats in each row. If you sit in the top few rows (Upper Bleacher, $12 face value tickets) you will be under the jumbotron scoreboard, which gives you some nice shade on a hot summer day. All the rows in the section are behind the Red Sox bullpen and Section 40. To calculate how many rows your seats are from the field, add 18 to the row number. So Row 20 is about 38 rows from the field, and so on. Keep in mind that you are also behind the bullpen.

Section 39

This section is much like Section 38 in that it is triangular and is behind Section 40 and the Red Sox bullpen. The rows in Section 39, however, face home plate. To calculate how many rows your seats are from the field, add 18 to the row number. So Row 20 is about 38 rows from the field, and so on. Keep in mind that you are also behind the bullpen

Section 40

An oddly-shaped little section, 40 is next to the centerfield triangle and down on the field. Some seats are on the warning track, and some are behind the Red Sox bullpen. Of all the bleacher sections, 40 is closest to the field.

There are 17 rows in this section, with between 2 and 27 seats per row. Some seats are on the warning track, and some are behind the Red Sox bullpen. Row 1 on the field, Row 2 is two rows off the field, and so on. Keep in mind that most of the seats in this section are also behind the bullpen.

Sections 41, 42, and 43

These three sections can rightfully be called the Right Field Bleachers, as opposed to Center Field Bleachers. All three sections have 49 rows, so there is a huge difference in being in the lower or upper sections of these sections. Section 41 is behind the Red Sox bullpen and 42 and 43 are behind the visitor's bullpen. With any of these sections, it is a good idea to get your seats above the fourth row. This is because there is a metal screen separating the bullpen from the bleachers and it affects your view if you are in the first few rows.

Sections 41 and 42 have 23 and 25 seats in each row, respectively, and Section 43 has 12 seats in each row. This makes Section 43 the easiest section for getting in and out of your seat for concessions and trips to the bathroom.

The famous "Red Seat," where Ted Williams hit the longest home run to stay inside Fenway Park, is Section 42, Row 37, seat 21.

For updated information about Fenway Park, ticket sales, the Fenway neighborhood, or to contact the author, visit this book's blog at **fenwayfanguide.com**